HEAL

OVERCOMING BULLYING, ABUSE, BURNOUT AND NEGLECT
ONE PIECE AT A TIME

BERNIE GIGGINS

DISCLAIMER

Copyright © 2018 **Bernie Giggins** All Rights Reserved.

The people and events described and depicted in this book are for educational purposes only. While every attempt has been made to verify information provided in this book, the author assumes no responsibility for any errors, inaccuracies or omissions.

If advice concerning medical matters is needed, the services of a qualified professional should be sought. This book is not intended for use as a source of medical advice.

The examples within this book are not intended to represent or guarantee that everyone or anyone will achieve their desired results. Each individual's success will be determined by his or her desire, dedication, effort and motivation. There are no guarantees you will achieve your desired outcome; the tools, stories and information are provided as examples only. All names have been changed to protect the identity of clients.

First Edition 2018 | Copyright 2018 by Bernie Giggins

All rights reserved. No part of this book may be reproduced, stored in a retrieval system or transmitted in any form by an electronic, mechanical, photocopying, recording means or otherwise without prior written permission of the publisher, Bernie Giggins.

TABLE OF CONTENTS

Introduction: Soul Journey: Core Belief Clearing 7

Chapter 1: My Life Before Heart And Soul Journey Connection 13

Chapter 2: Soul Wisdom To Begin Living The Life Of Your Dreams! 21

Chapter 3: Burnout Can Flow Into Compassion Fatigue 33

Chapter 4: Long-term Effects Of Bullying, Abuse And Neglect From Childhood 41

Chapter 5: Self-Compassion And Self-Love Re-Kindled 53

Chapter 6: Steps To Self-Love And Self-Compassion 61

Chapter 7: Essential Oils To Live Again By Young Living 71

Chapter 8: Chakras – Universal Life Force Centres 79

Chapter 9: Journalling Back Your Soulful Life 85

Chapter 10: Ho'oponopono Prayer Making Right Within 93

Chapter 11: Meditation – Letting Go And Surrendering To Soul 97

Chapter 12: When I Loved Myself Back Together Again 103

Chapter 13: Living A Soulful Life, Ever After! 107

About The Author 111

Testimonials And Case Studies 116

***

'The Soul always knows what to do to heal itself. The challenge is to silence the mind.' Caroline Myss

***

'In every moment, the Universe is whispering to you. You're constantly surrounded by signs, coincidences, and synchronicities, all aimed at propelling you in the direction of your destiny. Listen to your Soul, for it loves the Truth'. - Denise Linn

***

'The truth is, no matter what your current circumstances, if you can imagine something better for yourself you Can create it'. - John Assaraf

***

This book is dedicated to my soul mate and husband, Laurie, without your love, support and devotion, I would not be where I am today, thank you for being my rock.

To our children and their spouses, Wayne and Sonia, Jess and Adam, Brett and Jess, thank you for your love, I am so very proud of you all.

And our grandchildren Chase, Ava, Van, Jade, Chet and Eli thank you for bringing such joy, spontaneous love and laughter into our lives.

***

When I loved myself enough...

I found my voice and wrote this book for me to encourage you to

do the same by either writing or expressing your 'truth' out of

your mind and body.

***

Scan this QR Code to view my website and easily contact me anytime.

INTRODUCTION
SOUL JOURNEY: CORE BELIEF CLEARING

Are you always looking for approval, acceptance, inner peace or love?

Have you been betrayed, abused, bullied, abandoned or rejected in the past?

Are there repeating life patterns that you don't understand?

What you believe, consciously or subconsciously, is what you WILL receive in life. And this is especially true for childhood beliefs.

Our cellular memory locks in images and emotions of any negative or traumatic event, at any time in our lives, and stores them in the cells within our bodies. The damaged cells do not regenerate and stay continually damaged until you consciously clear and heal the memory. If not healed, it affects all areas of your life and will stay in your body as dis-ease, pain and negative beliefs or mindset. These are the cause of your current problems and repeating patterns. It remains on autopilot replay.

Our first memories are from childhood, between 0-7yrs, and will repeat subconsciously and automatically over our lifetime. The **Wounded Inner Child** becomes the saboteur in your life, repeatedly attracting to you the same lack of love or trust, rejection, failure or abandonment lesson you need to learn to clear and heal. It is a magnetic imprint of each negative experience.

Being bullied as a child will magnetise you repeatedly back into situations of bullying throughout your life, where you will be bullied, will protect others who are being bullied because someone didn't protect you as a child, or sometimes you even become the bully.

The negative core beliefs and messages are from the Wounded Inner Child. They are all subconsciously held, waiting to be healed. Michael Jackson had negative beliefs of not being good enough, that haunted him to his death; Lady Gaga has childhood memories of bullying still haunting her life today. Robin Williams, Whitney Houston, the list goes on.

The Soul Journey Core Belief Clearing session helps you connect with your wounded inner child, accessing the childhood memory, beliefs and messages causing the repeating problems in your life. The inner child is then allowed to express fully the truth and emotions suppressed at that time and age, in a safe and protected way, on a Soul level.

During this sacred clearing and healing ceremony, you, the adult self, acknowledge the hurt and give your inner child the resources they didn't have or receive at that time.

The phrase, "If I knew back then what I know now, my life would be completely different", gives you a second chance to positively change that past memory on a Soul and cellular level and all within the Soul circle of Truth.

Forgiveness, healing and karma happen to all concerned; you are now disconnected from all that once held you prisoner to the past. After the session, you'll feel free, lighter, inner peace and calm, your response and reactions to future situations will also change. You are re-connected to your own true Self to live your best life without regrets, your body and life start to heal and manifest your desires. Most clients are tired after their session as the war zone in their head is now at peace – no more internal struggling or fighting.

What wounded inner child memory is a skeleton in your memory closet, haunting you and causing problems in your life? What have you never told anyone before about your past? Imagine having a second chance to live in freedom and happiness to do, to be, to have without judgment, criticism or regret.

There's no need to imagine. As Nike says, "Just do it!"

When you're sick and tired of talking about the past and are ready for a new beginning in your life, try a Soul Journey Core Belief Clearing session.

To get started, contact me for a free 20-minute Healing Assessment - http://bit.ly/2u7vf1j

THE SOUL LOVES THE TRUTH!
The first 7 years of our growth are crucial. The influence of parents, family, and friends is powerful and anything good or bad will lock into our cellular memory. It holds us in repeating negative patterns subconsciously, that until we acknowledge and change, will remain on automatic replay.

As children, through different experiences, we were betrayed, abandoned, emotionally neglected by those we trusted to protect us. Then later on, we unwittingly abandoned and rejected our own Innermost self, our inner child. These are fragmented parts of ourselves, sometimes called dark or shadow parts, we have pushed away, disowned according to what others have dictated to us about what is 'acceptable' or not in this world.

Because of this, we live life doing for others what our inner child yearns to have done for us.

The childhood wounds can make us focus outwards on the opinions of others and we develop a need to seek approval and acceptance. Therefore we cannot maintain healthy, loving relationships, and form a habit of looking for mother or father figures in others to complete our life – searching for whatever is missing from our heart in our childhood.

Whatever is locked in or out of our heart as a child, and despite our best intentions, desires or strategizing to bring more of what we want into our life, later on, we have no receptor sites to allow it in. This makes it impossible for you to fully receive the person's loving intentions and allow them into your heart.

We search for inner peace, happiness or love, but when we get it, we cannot describe it, open fully to it or hold onto it because we never knew what it was to begin with.

It didn't matter how much or hard I tried, I could never receive the level of love I needed to fill the void of the childhood emotional neglect I experienced. I have since learned my mum did love me the best way she could, but my inner child had any love locked outside my heart and could never receive it. Now that I understand this, I am able to forgive myself for holding onto these negative memories for so long, only bringing regret and loss into my life.

I've had clients who have broken up with their partner or spouse, completed their Core Belief Clearing sessions and have reunited with the same person with a deeper love. They were closed to it before and now are open to give and receive. They realized the childhood memory they were stuck repeating had kept the image and experience of that past core belief memory, projecting it onto their partner or spouse, reminding them of the personality who originally hurt them.

Core Belief sessions allow you to move from self-abandonment, self-rejection and self-sabotage to self-compassion, self-love and self-acceptance. It allows us to accept from others what we could not give to ourselves first. You can only receive from others and life, what you are willing to give to your own self. When we resolve our inner misperceptions, our outer lives move back into harmony and balance.

Thank you for connecting with my book. There is a stirring within you that is searching for something more, wanting to heal yourself, to find that missing part inside.

You'll learn about my journey of unbecoming and undoing many years of living negative core beliefs, not truly understanding its effects on my adult life. I knew I was here on earth for something much bigger but didn't know how to change course and who to trust.

A huge wakeup call came with the death of my hero brother, which changed my life and direction forever. That's when I decided I didn't have to settle for less anymore, I found my voice and freedom to live my soul purpose with passion. I was guided to the teachers who could share their Soul knowledge and wisdom of ages with me, as well as the teachers to help me meet and make peace with my own inner child I had abandoned long ago.

In chapter 4, you'll learn about what I did to change the emotional 'self-harm' I had learned to survive life. I call it an emotional stroke and had to re-learn how to feel and express all my range of emotions, and to feel safe doing so. I had been running away from my soul's guidance instead of being led by my soul.

In chapter 6, you'll read how the death of my brother, my hero, guided me to change and stand up to my parents, entitled siblings and work bullies. What I had to undo and unbecome to be released from this curse from my childhood.

In chapter 7, you'll read what I did to release the negative 'stories' my mind genie replayed on autopilot, which gave me false validation of past negative childhood beliefs. How forgiveness, starting within me and then expanding outwards to others, has changed my world.

In chapter 8, I'll share what happened after reparenting my own Inner Child. All sorts of miracles began happening. I had an amazing relationship with my mother-in-law, as if our past was deleted. I received a redundancy from the corporate workplace where I was bullied and intimidated for so many years. Friends and family were more loving, positive and supportive and I had a voice first time in too many years to mention.

I share with you what I did to overcome the childhood bullying, abuse and emotional neglect which spiralled out of control in my adult life leading to burnout and compassion fatigue.

It's my aim to help you understand it doesn't have to be a life sentence of suffering from childhood hurts and traumas, guilt and shame, keeping us stuck in this cycle and not able to be released and set free. It has taken me many years to untangle myself from the layers of lies and stories to be who I am today, and now I want to help guide you to get there far more quickly.

Let's get started with helping you reach that freedom and inner peace within. To find your soulmate or fulfilling career. To climb the ladder of success, personally and financially, instead of remaining in the whirlpool you're in now. To have satisfaction instead of fatigue.

I've been there and can help you through to the other side, seeing life with new eyes and a different point of view, rather than the view you have seen so far.

I'm looking forward to meeting the part of you which has been locked away, never to be seen or heard, until now.

CHAPTER 1
MY LIFE BEFORE HEART AND SOUL JOURNEY CONNECTION

Before you begin to read this chapter, there's something you need to know. This was my mindset for many years – repeating the same patterns, habits and behaviours and hoping something would change. The definition of insanity. I think I had to be a little insane to survive the life I had. I felt like I was under a spell or curse and unable to break free.

By sharing my story with you, I hope you can get the message long before I did. We create our world by what we deeply believe about ourselves, subconsciously, on the inside. The people on the outside are our teachers, they are a mirror reflecting the beliefs we hold deep in our energy field. They are a surrogate of the personality we hadn't dealt with in the past.

I had unconscious beliefs that I wasn't strong enough, pretty enough or lovable enough for my mother. On the outside people bullied me to make me feel weak, *not strong enough* to say no or stop. I didn't realise until later these experiences were my spiritual learnings.

The bible says, "You reap what you sow". What was sown by our parents and other adults (negative or positive) in our childhood, is what we're reaping now, like it or not. We didn't ask for it and we didn't deserve it, but it's now time to reparent your own inner child, clear the old 'weeds' and sow the seeds you choose to reap in the weeks, months and years ahead.

Sow the seeds of kindness, love, gentleness, courage, abundance, whatever you didn't receive back then, you have the power within you to do this now.

We're all souls having an earthly experience. Our Soul is here on earth to learn lessons, to be of service, and to share our talents and gifts with others. We need to understand what the lessons are so we can learn and evolve to the next level to allow the door of opportunity to open for us to walk through.

MY FAMILY'S NEGATIVE INFLUENCE

I remember when I was 5 years old I knew I would never be able to live up to my mother's expectations of me.

I was one of eleven children in a strict Catholic family trying to make a living on a farm. We experienced extremes from abundance to struggling to make ends meet, which gave little security and no certainty. I was often in trouble for saying or doing the wrong thing but was not given guidance on how to do better, nor shown patience as I tried to figure it out on my own.

I felt I wasn't heard or validated, and when I shared my deep pain of severe bullying at junior and high school where children openly mocked my big nose and other physical characteristics, I was simply told to turn the other cheek and forgive.

There was no comfort, no protection, no help.

So, I learned a different way to cope with the taunts of bullies, even from my siblings. I instinctively numbed my emotions not to react, as any attention gave the bully more ammunition for me to be their puppet. I dug my fingernails into the palms of my hands to cause pain and stop the flow of tears, shutting down any emotional reaction. It began to work for me and I was released from the regular taunts for a while.

This was a survival technique. I didn't realise the real pain it would cause later in life and what it would ultimately cost me (an emotional stoke). To me, being emotional was a sign of weakness, a sign I wasn't good enough to be liked, accepted or to belong to a group.

My mother's harsh criticism and angry retorts quickly taught me not to voice my true thoughts and feelings. This lead to bottling up emotions that inevitably resulted in an explosion. I was chastised and bullied into 'the right family way'. Told off with 'how dare you' or segregated until I learned what was acceptable. I learned that receiving love, affection or attention came with conditions.

Later in life, speaking or hearing the word 'dare' would give me a 'nervous' body reaction of being electrically zapped. I couldn't work out why until I began discovering the layers of childhood emotional neglect hidden away.

The tone of voice, the punishment that followed, the shutdown of my emotions all wrapped up in that one word – *dare*. That was only one word, how many more words had their own connotation of punishment?

I learned I couldn't trust the family I was born into. Mum had divided the family; she had her favourites, the good ones, the entitled ones, while myself and four siblings were the leftovers.

Throughout my troubled teenage years, I learned to write my deepest secrets, fears and inner thoughts in my diary, which I locked. This helped release bottled up emotions. One afternoon I returned home, and mum had read my diary. I was in real trouble and faced more punishment. I never trusted myself to write again until my late thirties.

Emotionally I shut down over time and gave into the idea that I was there for others. I realized, heartbreakingly, they weren't there for me when I desperately needed them, then as well as later in life.

The time I could be myself was not within the family. It was with friends away from home. But I would be dobbed on, by a parent, back to my mother, for speaking my truth, saying what I felt or thought spontaneously in that moment, as a normal teenager would do. Then more punishment and lectures would follow, 'Ladies don't do or say that' blah, blah, blah.

Not having the mother-daughter bond, being segregated and never feeling good enough, resulted in me unconsciously seeking our mother-daughter connection. I would do anything to get that love from my mum, only to be emotionally hurt even more. The negative core belief had been stored, planted, and the family division had begun. I thought, surely, I wasn't that terrible not to be loved?

Over time, I became a people pleaser, hoping this would gain me the love, attention, and approval that was missing in my relationship with my Mother. Feeling like the black sheep of the family, I was the tomboy, the ADHD kid, getting the wrong attention for any trouble, I thought, 'One day, they'll tell me I'm adopted.' It was easier to accept a life as an orphan, the Cinderella in this family.

At 18, I left home to join the Women's Royal Australian Navy as a Dental Assistant and loved it. I could finally do what I wanted. I was free. Then at twenty I made a huge decision that would help my emotional and mental health with the bullying still happening within family and work.

I decided to change my nose. The source of decades of mockery and belittling.

The day before surgery I rang my mother. Instead of the support and comfort I'd hoped for, she criticized and yelled at me, accused me of insulting her and my father, and abused me for making the decision without their permission.

But I went ahead. It was the best decision I ever made!

I thought the bullying would end but I still attracted workplace bullying and insults from others. Looking back, the lesson I learned was that others were a mirror of what I deeply felt about myself. I felt I had betrayed my own self by 'cutting off my nose to spite others'. When in fact, I wanted to get away from other's negative comments and out of the spotlight. I felt I wasn't strong enough to defend or ignore their comments. I couldn't trust others if I did get a compliment as in the past, it was a joke on me. So, I learned to repel or laugh off compliments, not to appear gullible.

This warped belief system of 'not being good enough' carried into my marriage and put me at the mercy of a bullying mother-in-law who always got her own way. I had married her only son and I felt I paid the price for loving him. It would get to a point where I'd stand up to her, only to have it be my word against her word to the other members of my husband's family.

I learned it wasn't worth the animosity. Again, I emotionally numbed myself to her sarcasm and critical judgements. When I didn't react to her critical barbs, she would gossip to others who would pass on her cruel words to me, deepening the wound and entrenching the self-protective behaviours I'd learned to survive with my Mother. Yet again, I thought, 'Surely I wasn't that terrible not to be loved or accepted?'

My mother's negative influence had crushed any confidence or courage to start new ventures. I was crippled by fear of retaliation or someone challenging my actions and I couldn't stand up for myself.

It was only in my forties that I began to recover from a lifetime of bullying and abuse, to grieve the lost opportunities and freedom, and begin to heal that wound of emotional neglect. To thank my soul for protection and for keeping me alive to stay here on earth.

At work, I was in a managing role in one career and administration role in another and was being bullied by bosses. Not liking confrontation, I worked harder, but the bullying took its toll on my health and I ended up with many illnesses.

Yet I would always summon up any courage I had within me to stand up for anyone who was being bullied, to be the rock for them whenever they needed me. Many times to the detriment of my own health and wellbeing.

I was the 'unpaid counsellor' in whatever role I had in life; giving advice, consoling others, I had changed into an empathic personality. An empath is compassionate towards others, feeling the emotions not spoken by others and wanting to protect, fix or rescue others. This was because no one protected me as that little child, so my inner child was protecting others automatically and on autopilot.

We'll look at this more deeply in chapter 3, Burnout and Compassion Fatigue. It will show you how the suppressed negative emotional memories and core beliefs, if not cleared, can lead to burnout and compassion fatigue resulting in health and life challenges.

Because of many years of suppressing my emotions and not even allowing my young kids to see me cry, it physically, mentally and emotionally took its toll. Mentally I was always on guard, in protection mode for my children. I gave them what I never received – unconditional love, treating them equally and fairly, allowing them to experience life and accepting them as they were. I would do without, so they could have more than I ever received as a child.

Physically my pain threshold was extremely high, as I needed to be there for my children. I couldn't trust my mother or mother-in-law with them if something were to happen to me or my husband.

Even Mother's Day gave me angst. There wasn't a card I read that I wanted to give both mothers; maybe one with a wilted flower or a thistle on it?

I felt like a hypocrite. I was the mother to my children I didn't have, part of me was Joan of Arc, yet the other was addicted to seeking my mother's love and attention. I wanted to prove I was a 'good enough daughter'. What was wrong with me?

I felt there were two sides to me, the good, light side and the bad, dark side which was behind closed doors – self-critical, judgmental, self-sabotaging with low self-worth and no self-confidence.

THE TURNING POINT
I didn't connect to my soul and soul purpose until a few years after my parents died and only a few years before my mother-in-law passed away. I wished I'd known all this before that time. I could have a few happier memories to hold onto now. For those last couple of years with my mother-in-law, it was the best we had experienced in the thirty years I'd been married. Because I had cleared and changed these deep-seated negative memories, dissolved the old filters I was seeing life through, and reconnected to my inner child again, the outside world was mirroring back the happy, loving and carefree energy I now had on the inside.

I finished a course in Healing the Wounded Inner Child through the Akashic records. This course added to the Soul Coaching® and Journey practitioner courses I had trained in to access the deepest negative core beliefs and memories anchoring me to the past.

The more I thought and spoke of the past negative influences and experiences, the more I created and attracted it in my present world. Once I learned this new way of accessing, clearing and reconnecting to my inner child, I began a new life of ease, grace, inner peace and freedom, filled with unconditional love that was always around, just invisible to me.

My children are my greatest teachers. After learning Soul and Journey coaching and Core Belief clearing, I put it into practice to clear any negative memories from my past. I realised a lot of my own fears were projected onto my kids, controlling or suppressing them like I had been controlled. Thinking I knew best for them, rather allow to experience for their own self.

You are here in perfect divine timing. Everything happens for a reason in the spiritual and soul world. By reading my before-and-after journey, as well as the case studies of my clients, I hope it motivates you to act in releasing suppressed negative memories in your life.

My clients and I have all completely changed our lives and continue to do so, being able to access and follow our soul path again. Our spiritual soul path is always there, only sometimes it's invisible to us because of the negative core beliefs controlling and constricting our lives.

If you feel called, then reach out to me via my website or email, so you can begin to live and enjoy life with freedom and inner peace.

I enjoy life like never before, my senses are heightened, new people come into my life and abundance flows, and *you can have this too*.

I have been where you are now, and I can help you through or over the ravine that has disconnected you from living your life to the fullest.

CHAPTER 2

SOUL WISDOM TO BEGIN LIVING THE LIFE OF YOUR DREAMS!

This is a chapter I had written in 2012 for *Soul Whispers III*, a book about Soul Coaching®, personal stories by Soul Coaches of the world, and exercises to connect you deeply to your own soul. The Journey™ and Soul Coaching® allowed me to have a voice, one I wasn't used to as it had been shut down over the years, little by little. But now, Soul has guided me to experience the openness and courage to speak, write, and live my divine soul truth. This is my story of how Soul awoke my spirit to follow the guidance, Soul path, and synchronicities set out for me and I would like to share it with you now.

***

Have you ever wondered why you do things you never dreamt you would do? Have you repeatedly had dreams and visions about living in a different culture, and felt at home with people and cultures, vastly different from your own?

In my childhood, I loved the Native American Indians. I loved watching movies about them and got upset when and if the soldiers hurt or cheated the Indians. I felt their pride and was inspired by them, as if I were one of them. I related to them because they loved and respected the earth and animals just like I did.

I never understood this phenomenon as a child. Why did I feel so connected to them when I felt so alienated within my own family, who didn't understand me the way I felt the Indians would?

Decades later, I still had a strong yearning to finally meet and engage in conversation with Native American People. So, when I saw that a local intuitive counsellor was sponsoring two American Indian Elders to come to our city for a talk, I immediately jumped at the chance to attend this event.

I felt as though I was with family!

After that meeting, I went to the library to look for books to borrow, opening my heart to any signs pointing to which book or author might have wisdom to share that would be beneficial for my higher self.

A book titled, *Soul Coaching: 28 Days to Discover your Authentic Self* by Denise Linn popped up on the library computer screen. I thought to myself, "I don't have the time to sit down for an hour each day and do this work", but I trusted that this was the book I was guided to. So respectfully, I took it home and started preparing what was needed for the next 28 days.

Denise Linn's ancestry is Cherokee Indian, so I blessed her for this Native American link and the universal guidance which drew me to this book at this time in my life. Little did I know the book was to change my life forever.

I followed the guidance given in the book, the daily ritual Denise suggested, journal writing, noting what the universe was telling me, and really connecting myself to my creator, with no church between us, no lies and nothing kept hidden.

In the program, you make a commitment to the universe and its creator to complete the course. There are four parts that you work through in a specific order: mental-air; emotional-water; spiritual-fire; physical-earth. This process slowly strips away all the uncomfortable past, uncovering who said what, how it felt, everything that is authentic and specific, to you. The Soul truth and nothing but the Soul truth, so help me god.

I had committed to waking up early, to use the early morning hours as my time for completing the program before my children woke up. That way, I could really focus on clearing the chains that were holding me back to the past.

I remember so clearly day 11 of mental-air week. Early that morning as I was writing my daily journal, my daughter came to me with a dream she had of the future. It was a very upsetting dream that held echoes of things that had not been healed from my family's past. In that moment, I had to find a voice of confidence and authority to reassure her in no uncertain terms that nothing like what she had dreamed would ever happen in this lifetime.

I also knew in that moment, without a shadow of a doubt, that the past can and would be healed. By working through this Soul Coaching® book, I had discovered a new voice inside, one which now spoke with strength and love. It scared me at first and I thought I needed an exorcist – I wasn't used to using this voice of mine, who's was it!

This was a turning point in my life, and after completing the Soul Coaching® program, I knew I wanted to train with Denise Linn to become a Soul Coach, helping other souls to live the life of their dreams, to awaken their calling through clearing emotional baggage that wasn't theirs, by guiding them back through their past lives or this life to change their lives for the better.

After completing the Soul Coaching® book, I tried to find out whether Denise Linn would be coming to Australia again so I could continue more courses with her. I felt utter dejection when I realized the only way this could happen was if I travelled to see her in the USA. That night I tried so hard to imagine myself being on the plane, flying to her ranch and completing the course, feeling what it would be like. That's what the Law of Attraction says to do, right?

Through the night my ego head kicked in and said, "You can't go to America. You have school fees, a family to look after." This plunged my mind, with my soul underneath, into despair. I felt I was back where I started, stuck in the same way of life, not able to escape. This was hard to face, after having tasted the freedom my soul yearned for. But my mind was only replaying the story of my life so far - childhood betrayals, emotional neglect, being bullied, almost getting to the top and someone else taking the glory, having the rug pulled out from beneath me, being told, "You will be treated equally" only to have other given special treatment instead. It reminded me of my mother, my mother-in-law, and bosses.

This made me so upset, I continued crying and asking, "Why can't I go to the USA to do Denise Linn's Training and become a Soul Coach?"

But my soul had other things I needed to learn yet, if only I could trust. Trust can be difficult for any adult who has had their trust betrayed as a child.

The next day was a Mind, Body, and Soul Expo, which was my yearly outlet for Spiritual Guidance and healing, a gift I gave myself. While driving there I said, "If I can't go to America, then show me what else I am meant to do, thank you Soul!"

I met a wonderful Soul Coach called Maria Elita, there who is also a Crystal Bed Healer. Following my intuition, I had a couple of sessions with Maria, and then completed her practitioner course. Maria then introduced me to Scott Alexander King, an animal dreamer who lived with shamans and sages around the world to learn the wisdom he shares today.

Well, I thought, here's a shaman who's lived with Native Americans. Maybe I am to learn the way of the Australian Animal Dreaming? Meanwhile, I had not forgotten the commitment I had made back in June to attend Denise Linn's Soul Coaching® Training on her Ranch in the USA. So, every morning when I walked my dog, I would stand in front of the sunrise and ask Grandfather Sun to guide my direction towards Denise's Ranch, never giving up.

Three months later, my next-door neighbour was reading a book, and needed someone who she could trust to be her guide and mentor as she was going through the process. This meant that I had to read the book as well. I told her I didn't really have time to do this, but she continued asking and seemed so desperate, I felt obliged to read it.

I couldn't put the book down.

The Journey™, by Brandon Bays, was another book which took my body by the horns and allowed my soul to be free and to sing. And yes, I helped my neighbour with her process. With Reiki and dowsing modalities, we got to the root cause of her issue and cleared it.

Brandon Bays stirred my soul, so I attended a beginner class and was blown away with what was released from the closets of my childhood held in my cellular memory bank. I went to the next seminar of *The Journey* in October 2008.

Wow! I thought, here is another mentor who like Denise Linn, also believes that The Soul Loves the Truth and I was following the breadcrumbs of my Soul.

The next seminar was even more powerful, uncovering more childhood scars and healing them on a soul level. I felt so alive, so free and liberated. I knew I needed to complete Brandon Bays' courses and continue listening to my soul. But I had still not forgotten Denise Linn, or my commitment to meeting her. I continued saying my morning prayer to be guided towards her. But it wasn't meant to be at this time. So, I kept following the guidance of my soul, one piece, one step and one day at a time.

I noticed there was an Abundance course of *The Journey* coming up in two weeks' time. But it was in Perth, on the western coast of Australia. I had never been to that side of the continent or flown that far before. If I wanted to complete The Journey Practitioner Program now, I needed to do this course because there wasn't another one for at least six months.

But I had never left my family before, I was still working full time, and where was I going to find the money to travel a four-day journey to and from? All these fears kept rising inside of me, but my soul's yearning was even greater. I knew I had to put my intentions out into the universe and trust that my family and I would be looked after.

I was committed. So that's what I did.

I told my husband, who possibly thought I was crazy, that I was going. I checked the flights and got the latest as it was the cheaper one. I got the time off work which was a little harder, but I persisted, and I confidently asked The Journey Office for a Payment Plan - all okay - so all systems go!

Did I mention that I'm extremely shy with strangers, an introvert, a person of a few words unless it's something I'm passionate about? But even so, I kept following my soul's guidance, and everything was falling into place easily without my interference.

The Abundance Course produced amazing results. It uncovered more untruths about my identity and childhood wounds. How many more were there in my attic or buried in the basement? Over the next year, I was changing and blossoming into my own true self, still following my soul guidance.

An old friend I hadn't seen for many years wanted to know if I'd had a face life, saying I looked so much younger and more vibrant! I told her, "No, I just got rid of years of emotional baggage that wasn't mine and time to ditch!"

In the next twelve months, I was guided to learn and follow the teachings of Florence Skovel Shinn through two of her books, *Your Word is Your Wand* and *The Game of Life and How to Play it*. I was learning that you are what you say you are, and I now realize the energy behind what we think and speak.

I am forever careful and now remind others that we have become lazy and take for granted what we say and do, not realizing the power of words and thoughts attract the same. Florence's teachings and affirmations also assist us in connecting our soul to the creator.

Another powerful book is, *The Secret Language of the Body* by Inna Segal, which teaches us that whatever we cannot express or clear can manifest into physical ailments. I was led to follow Inna's teachings which taught how to read and communicate with the body and inner wisdom; sharing the underlying causes of illness and disease, how to release to self-heal, helping to uncover the negative thoughts, energy and emotions affecting the body, mind and being. I am now one of Inna's Visionary Intuitive Practitioners, healing myself and now my clients through listening to those 'secret messages of the body'.

But back to my Dream Goal of meeting Denise Linn...

I'd put this on the back burner as in my mind I had overspent on other courses, completing whatever else I needed to do. Yet I was still saying my intention every morning on my walk and leaving it up to the gods.

My soul yearning kept calling, and in October 2009, I decided I wanted to attend Denise's class in May 2010. So, I sent my deposit and made the commitment to go. I had to keep my word to myself to honour my commitment to soul.

In January 2010, I couldn't get time off work to go to the USA, so I rang to cancel my booking. Denise answered the phone. Since I was now talking to my mentor, my heart skipped a beat and my soul connected. I felt blessed. I then talked to Meadow, Denise's Daughter. I told her I didn't want a refund as I WOULD be attending another time. She asked me if I was interested in coming in September 1st to 9th that year to a course that was not yet advertised. Feeling the Numerology as another positive sign, I said, "Yes! Book me in and I will see you in September."

Such conviction! I even surprised myself at how much I had changed since April 2008. I was grateful I had followed my soul's guidance to get where I am and become who I was meant to be.

Having now committed to going to the USA in September 2010, I opened my heart up for the signs and guidance I needed from soul. I have learned that when I try to control the outcome and live in my head, it makes it so much harder for my dreams to come true. When I surrender it up to my soul, live in, and speak from my heart, everything falls into place and works out better than I could have ever imagined. When I hear these words, I know that soul has taken care of the details and the outcome.

I completed the Journey Practitioner course in March 2010, with huge changes in and around me on all levels. During this 18-month course, I met a friend who was also interested in meeting Denise Linn and who said she would love to go with me. She asked if I wanted to travel around Italy with her and her children on the way back from California. This would mean being overseas for a whole month, by far the longest I had been away from my husband and family.

The fears started to creep in again… What about the money? Getting time off work? I couldn't speak Italian and didn't really know this woman I was going to travel with… But I kept breathing in God's Will and breathing out my will, trusting that everything would work out by my soul's perfection.

Looking back on it now, it was incredible how my soul, behind the scenes and beneath the surface, was weaving an amazing story and unfolding it effortlessly. It reminds me of Moses parting the Red Sea without effort. My husband started taking over my role, without being asked; the kids started asking him for advice and also taking more responsibility; work offered me a higher position for 6 weeks before I left; connections were made overseas; the travel agent offered unbelievable discounts; the timing was worked out to a tee for meeting with my friend's children in Rome for the drive around Italy for eight days and then four days by ourselves with friends of friends.

Another of Denise Linn's sayings is, "Beneath the surface, it's happening."

Wow, wasn't that the truth! I know now to just leave things out of my mind and back in my heart, and everything works out perfectly.

We arrived in California for the Soul Coaching® and Past Life Regression Course. When I reached the Labyrinth at the top of the hill overlooking Denise Linn's Property, I gave thanks to Grandfather Sun, the universe, and to my soul for bringing me to Summerhill Ranch.

What a moment to remember and be grateful for! I was living the life of my dreams by following the guidance of my soul. In California, the sun sets into the ocean, whereas where I live in Australia, it rises over the ocean. So on the Labyrinth at Summerhill, I felt like I had reached the other end of the Rainbow. I gave thanks, feeling so grateful and so blessed for my soul's journey so far, with more to come.

The ranch, teachings, friendships made, and memories taken were more than I could have imagined or ever dreamed of. I learned that I was an Indian Brave in a Past Life, giving the connection to my childhood. On the day of leaving the ranch, I was sad. But inside I was so excited and proud. A new spark of my soul had awoken.

Italy! I couldn't sleep past 2.30am because of the Jet Lag, so I would sit in the bathroom and read or write in my journal until daylight. Then the days of sightseeing would begin. I felt like a little kid, in awe of everything, absolutely savouring every moment, every minute, as I didn't know if I would ever come this way again. I was like an ADHD child - here, there and everywhere at once, walking so fast, seeing as much as I could, knowing that what I saw was enough for me, not having regrets of what I didn't do, taking more than enough photos, but knowing that I could never reclaim that moment again, honouring the time my soul had given me, here and now.

Every day I said my intention that, "I allow whatever my soul needs me to hear, see, feel or know today and I will accept it all."

As a child, for as long as I can remember, I had been bullied and emotionally neglected by my parents, especially my mother. Then I changed myself into the people-pleaser to 'fit in', making sure others had happy memories, they felt loved and heard, and were given whatever I had to give. I forgot about me and my own needs, longing for others to return the favour. Sometimes they did, but I couldn't accept it or didn't know how to, as that was how my mind was programmed throughout childhood.

This dream trip to train with Denise Linn helped me to find myself, stand up for myself, allow myself my own freedom to choose what and whom I like and don't like. This was the dream trip of a lifetime for me, and I made the most of it, without regret.

Denise Linn's training has taught me that I am not my identity. The one given to me by my parents, family, friends, school, career, life, etc. Who I truly am is much more magnificent, remarkable and eternal. I have learned not to judge these patterns ingrained into me, simply observing and accepting this part of me. My "Soul Loves the Truth" and I know that by following my soul, I will achieve inner peace to be myself, not what others expect me to be.

While on the trip, I became stubborn when I needed to, not wanting to be led or to follow others if I didn't want to. I wanted to make this my time and my journey, to not have regrets and resentment when I returned to Australia - that I didn't do, see or touch this or that when I was there in that space and time.

I even spoke up to dominating people, though I was quivering inside, knowing I was fighting for my trip, my time, my money, and not accepting other people's excuses to have their choice over mine. I wasn't afraid anymore. The changes that happened have continued to be part of my life.

Wow, how I have changed from the person I once was to who I am now! I believe my Soul guided all the events to connect my earthly heart to Soul Coaching® and the Journey™, leading me back to my soul path and purpose here on earth. As much as I didn't like being slowed down before attending Denise Linn's USA certification course, I needed to learn the Journey® and have my stored up negative core belief memories vault cleared and healed to have space to comprehend Soul Coaching®. Which I am forever grateful to my Soul!

During all these changes since 2008, many people around me were separating and divorcing, some friends drifting away, with new positive supportive friends coming into my life. My husband was getting concerned that we would follow the same path of separation. I told him these people had been living another identity and not being true to themselves, that I wouldn't ever stay in this marriage if I didn't love him or in any other relationship, I would never sell my soul to the devil and live a dead existence, ever again.

My husband and children respect and support what I learn, live, love and do; they witness and like my positive changes and the changes in my clients. After years since the beginning of my real soul journey, beginning with reading Denise Linn's book, we are coming up to 36 years of marriage, more abundant in every way we choose, and life is unfolding through our dreams and goals daily.

Our yacht is called Dream'n'On. We bought her, just before I started my Soul Journey connection. Synchronistic events brought her into our life at the time, and it felt like another sign when I saw the name. My husband loves to sail her, and I love to relax and recharge my energy while on her. On every trip I thank her for being in our life.

***

When I loved myself enough...

I forgave myself for all the times I thought I wasn't good enough, in the eyes and opinions of others. I learned to find my tribe where I was 'safe' to be and express who I am. - KimMcMillen

***

CHAPTER 3
BURNOUT CAN FLOW INTO COMPASSION FATIGUE

Burnout is a term that has been used since the early 1980s. It's used describe the physical and emotional exhaustion that workers can experience when they have low job satisfaction and feel powerless and overwhelmed at work.

However, burnout does not necessarily mean that our view of the world has been damaged, or that we have lost the ability to feel compassion for others.

The long-term stress from burnout is exhausting and can prevent you from taking part in activities that you normally find meaningful. While I was at work, the cutbacks put extra burdens on the staff still employed. Then add more stress to that with bullying and intimidation within toxic working environments and it brought out the fight within me to stand up to the managers. I had an attitude of, "You won't force me out, I'm staying!" I needed the money.

Burnout can be easily resolved. Taking leave, having a holiday or changing jobs can provide immediate relief to someone suffering from job-related burnout. But not me! My next job always started off confident and passionate but soon turned into me taking on more responsibilities than others or being the target for bullies. Did I have a sign on my back that said, 'pick on me'? As a supervisor I would stand up for the younger staff when needed to against the managers.

These were all repeating habits, patterns and behaviours I needed to address, or they would continue to rule my life, automatically and on autopilot. I was hitting the same wall repeatedly and ending up in the same situation and with the same health problems.

I realized my old core belief memory was unconsciously overstepping the boundaries of others. I would stand up for anyone who was being bullied, anyone who needed it, whether they asked or not. This also related to my own family and friends. Looking back, I assumed and stepped in, being the good Samaritan, unconsciously giving to them, I now realized, because no one helped or protected me back when I was younger. But I was the one left with the emotional, physical and mental trauma while the other person who was being bullied or intimidated, was fine. I didn't learn my lesson, so it kept repeating.

I HAVE SINCE LEARNED
My emotional shut down from childhood, which created a fear of failure and fear of rejection, kept me burning the candle at both ends, in whichever role I was in. My self-diagnosed 'attention deficit hyperactive disorder' (ADHD) energy was very high. I would work all day and at that time when my kids were small, I loved cake decorating as a hobby on the side. The only peace and quiet was when they were asleep. So, I would be creating amazing cake designs until 3am sometimes, have a couple of hours sleep and be up when my kids woke up. Not a problem! Or so I thought.

Looking back, I was very hard on myself. I didn't respect or honour my body by continually doing these extra hours of excessive tasks. It was like shift work and my fears and core beliefs ran my life without me realizing it until many years later. There was no self-compassion or self-love. Just pushing myself to keep up, not wanting to fail or let others down. This was unconsciously driving my behaviour.

Stop and listen to your body. What are the messages it's getting your attention for? I had a list of health problems, drug prescriptions, specialist appointments, time off work for serious illness, the list goes on. This was all at the height of bullying and intimidation within my work environment. Then I connected heart to Soul Coaching® and Journey method®, the Secret Language of your Body and I learned self-compassion and self-love and started using Young Living essential oils and supplements (more on all this later). Today, I have no health problems and I'm called only to attend yearly medical examinations.

COMPASSION FATIGUE

I didn't know about Compassion Fatigue Syndrome (CFS) until I was discussing a new client's details with the manager of a coaching company I was contracted to. She mentioned this syndrome and it hit me that the Soul Journey Core Belief Clearing sessions with my clients were actually dissolving the symptoms and memories of CFS permanently.

Compassion Fatigue Syndrome is a form of post-traumatic stress that develops as an indirect response to someone else's suffering. It is the 'compulsive and automatic concern for the needs of others while ignoring your own needs.' 99% of caring people are empath personalities. Empaths are highly sensitive, can feel other people's energies and want to change, save, rescue or take away their pain. They can easily be taken advantage of by their own kind nature or unresolved suppressed emotional memories.

"Empath personalities are earth angels and are needed in life. They are here to feel and clear dark emotions from the collective. Speeding up the return of light for the planet. It is a profound service for which empaths were born." - Matt Kahn, Whatever Arises, Love That.

People who work in "helping professions" daily and/or are called to respond to individual, community, national, and even international crises are being exposed daily to the sights and sounds of trauma, pain, abuse, neglect. The things you see and hear which you cannot delete. Helpers, volunteers and carers may also feel a negative effect associated with their ability to help and not be able to change the situation of the person they care for. These are all experiencing CFS.

It can also affect parents or a partner, wife or husband wanting to make the marriage work, make the family work, make the relationship with the child work. Domestic violence, dysfunctional families, all can have lasting effects from burnout to compassion fatigue. One of these partners will always be an empath personality, the rescuer, fixer, protector or changer.

I researched CFS and sure enough, the unresolved and unexpressed childhood memories and core beliefs were directly related to people suffering from CFS, myself included. This is what I had while working in the toxic environments and toxic family, I couldn't give up or disconnect from. Then as a healer and empath, I was connected 24/7 to my clients' needs without realizing the consequences.

Once I learnt this, I became conscious of my connection to the client, took time for my own needs, allowing the client to heal at their own pace. I learned to honour their life journey, accept them as they are. I am not God, so I stopped trying to play his role.

Stop being the martyr to others, this is unhealthy empathic behaviour. The work, person, job, becomes the 'project' for the empath, thinking they can change, save or fix the 'project'. But it doesn't matter how many times the 'project' fails to improve, the empath gives more excuses. The story of my life?

A person with negative core beliefs or limiting beliefs which keep them in a repeating habit, pattern or behaviour throughout their life is prone to be a compassionate fatigue candidate.

Many of my clients don't realize the reason they're in their career or volunteering is because subconsciously they want and need to protect, save, rescue, or change others before themselves. The person's unconscious childhood memory controls their behaviour and their life.

Have you ever been willing to put your life on the line for others? Do you put your heart and soul into your life, work, clients, patients, students or animals? Have you ever cared so deeply about someone it hurt you to see them suffer? Of course, you have because you are compassionate, sympathetic and nurturing, it's part of our human nature.

Emotional depletion, a side effect of compassion fatigue, can be caused by taking your 'work' home with you; determining your own value by the outcome of your clients and the ongoing drain of hearing stories of sadness and struggle. Just don't let it control your life.

The risk of emotional depletion can be modified by emotional resiliency (self-care and be able to switch off the compassion emotion) and developing coping or problem-solving skills. When you're aware of the side effects, you have a choice and chance to change your daily patterns and habits to a healthier, beneficial life for you.

As the airline stewardess advises us, put the oxygen mask on yourself first before helping anyone else. This will keep you in compassion or job satisfaction instead of fatigue or depletion.

IS COMPASSION FATIGUE OR BURNOUT CONTROLLING YOUR LIFE?

This can relate to career, relationships, money, love, religion, children, partner, volunteering, anything.

- Why did you choose that profession or partner, or why did it (or they) choose you?
- Is your career giving you satisfaction or are you feeling let down?
- Can you switch off, stop thinking about your work or relationship?
- What or who will you never give up on in life? What is this costing you?

- What difference do you want to make in the world? Is it because of your childhood, and have you completed that for your own self yet?

THE FIRST STEPS TO SUCCESS AND BEING RELEASED FROM CFS:
- Become aware of what an 'empath' is.
- Recognise the default patterns your behaviour follows.
- Put personal boundaries in place. You need to own, feel and be responsible for dealing with your own pain, unresolved childhood pain and past life pain first.
- A healthy empath knows how to give unconditional love and care without being hooked into becoming the imprisoned slave or martyr.

I had to learn to let go of:
- The need to be a people pleaser
- Enabling someone's destructive behaviour by making excuses for them
- Doing other people's work for them
- Being the martyr or scapegoat for other people's unresolved traumas
- Forcing myself to spend time with people out of a sense of duty, guilt or to uplift them
- Giving energy to people who were not respectful of my feelings or my time
- The addiction to being a victim, repeating the bullying and abuse cycle unconsciously

I HAVE SINCE LEARNED
A few years ago, a dear close friend of mine was on life support. I had only just learned Reiki energy healing modality after soul coaching. Morning and night, I prayed for her to live, to stay here on

earth because her husband and three little children needed her here.

I sent distant Reiki to her body and soul and I was becoming exhausted. I meditated and realized spiritually I was overstepping my boundaries. I was *willing* her to live without respecting her soul path and soul journey wishes.

I then changed the prayers and Reiki to support her soul's journey and wishes, to live or to pass over, I would honour her. Within twenty-four hours she passed over and I received a sign from her soul soon after. This was a turning point for me and my Soul Journey career for being a servant of my God.

When you're giving your heart and soul to your career or loved ones, there is a point in time which compassion 'fatigue' is switched on. Spiritually, you become closed off and your life force drains.

Luckily, Compassion Fatigue can be identified, stopped and treated at any stage – the sooner, the better!

What I know for sure in my soul business is that unresolved emotional memories and core beliefs from your past set you up to be an ideal candidate for CFS.

Because the core belief memory hasn't been cleared, you're still attached to the power of it, making the original negative experience to come true, repeatedly attracting the same personalities and experiences.

Our bodies are like a car – if we don't look after it, change the oil, put in fuel, pump air in the tyres, we run the risk of breakdowns, also run it into the ground.

Now, from this day forward, I would like you to think about your body as if it's an electric car. It has to be recharged at certain times, every day. When it stops, it stops. No pushing or jumper leads to get more kilometres out of it.

Don't let the core beliefs of you being responsible, of needing to fix, rescue or change others, control your present life.

Are you falling into old habits or patterns, forgetting about your Inner Child and their needs?

Are you constantly giving more to others? Struggling with lack, pain and unable to receive or fill up your energy tanks?

Is there an area of your health or life beginning to fall apart?

At the end of the book I will be giving case studies. These share with you my clients' before-and-after stories of their Soul Journey Core Belief Clearing sessions.

While we are still under the spell of the core belief, we cannot live to our fullest potential. If you don't know, then you can't grow, if you can't feel then you cannot heal and release the past. Some of our beliefs have been buried for so long, we can't remember. As you read, connect with your body and heart. Feel if the story 'reminds' you of anything in the past.

Clients will say they are getting on so well with their parent/s now that they don't want to jeopardise the relationship now. My answer is, the Core belief memory is not about now, it is about the age when the memory occurred, and the age that adult was. You need to connect with that age and memory for any resolution to ever occur and complete.

If you are experiencing lack, struggle, pain, loss or other negatives emotions, then read on.

> *"When looking for a therapist or coach, check out their background, they may have credentials, but have they cleared and healed their own childhood wounds? Someone who has not done his/her own emotional healing grief work cannot guide you through yours. No one can lead you somewhere that they haven't been."* - John Bradshaw

CHAPTER 4
LONG-TERM EFFECTS OF BULLYING, ABUSE AND NEGLECT FROM CHILDHOOD

What happens to us in early life has a huge impact on us in later life, until WE change it. We cannot rely on anyone outside of our mind and body here on earth to do this for us – it's an inside job. Our body remembers everything that has ever happened to us, it cannot speak to us, and it can only gain our attention by connecting with us through our senses. That's why we react to certain smells, sounds, feelings, sights and nerves which trigger the memory to be cleared.

To help you understand more about the lasting effect of being programmed, conditioned, brainwashed, repeatedly abused from childhood, I'm going to tell you about Ivan Pavlov and his dogs.

The famous Pavlov's Dog experiments helped me to understand a little of how my negative childhood influence could keep me under a spell, not be able to breakthrough.

Ivan Pavlov was a Russian scientist interested in studying how digestion works in mammals. He observed and recorded information about dogs and their digestive process. As part of his work, he began to study what triggers dogs to salivate which in turn established some principles of classical conditioning. The conditioning concerns 'learned' or conditioned behaviour.

We all have behaviours that we seek to change. The Pavlov's Dogs illustration helps us to understand more about why we respond 'irrationally' to certain situations.

It provides a true example for anyone seeking to understand how our past experiences can prompt certain behaviours in the future, for example, fear of public speaking, heights, flying, being reprimanded or tested, etc.

The initial Pavlov's Dogs experiment was simply to place a dog in a controlled environment. The people who fed Pavlov's dogs wore lab coats. Pavlov noticed that the dogs began to drool whenever they saw lab coats, even if there was no food in sight. Pavlov wondered why the dogs salivated at lab coats, and not just at food. He ran a study in which he rang a bell every time he fed the dogs. Pretty soon, just ringing a bell made the dogs salivate.

The simple experiment established that the dogs did not need the food to respond to food. They were responding to a stimulus or 'trigger' that produced the same response as the real thing. Pavlov could make the dog salivate whenever the lab coat or sound was seen or heard and without food being present.

He summed it up like this: there's a *neutral* stimulus (the bell), which by itself will not produce a response, like salivation. There's also a non-neutral or *unconditioned stimulus (the food),* which will produce an *unconditioned response (salivation).* But if you present the neutral stimulus and the unconditioned stimulus together, eventually the dog will learn to associate the two. After a while, the neutral stimulus by itself will produce the same response as the unconditioned stimulus, like the dogs drooling when they hear the bell. This is called a *conditioned response*.

Think of an unconditioned response as completely natural and a *conditioned* response as something that we learn, which can become deeply embedded and well established over time.

Whatever reaction you had to abuse, bullying or neglect during childhood becomes a *conditioned response*. You learn to experience anxiety, depression, numbness, or disease as a response (into your nervous system) and this then repeats throughout your whole life, until YOU access and change it.

Any repeated bullying, abuse, or neglect from childhood have a serious impact on mental wellbeing, with victims more prone to anxiety, depression, suicidal tendencies, low mood, disturbed sleep, reduced confidence and problems with low self-esteem and low self-worth.

Victims are usually, consciously or unconsciously, searching for safety, survival and security and most times are taken advantage of by the same 'personality trait' as the person who hurt or harmed them in childhood.

It can also trigger a range of physical health problems, from aches and pains to increased susceptibility to infections and digestive upset. Experiencing harassment at home, school, community or work can leave you more vulnerable to long-term ill-health.

"He who angers you, controls you."

Exposure to stress triggers a series of physical changes within your body, known as the fight-or-flight response, designed to protect you from danger. In its simplest terms, when your brain recognises a stressful situation, it stimulates the release of a hormone adrenaline, which encourages your kidneys to release epinephrine. This in turn triggers the release of the stress hormone cortisol, which raises your blood pressure and pulse, increases your blood sugar levels and prepares your muscles for action, while suppressing less essential processes such as immune and digestive function.

The list of health dysfunctions that stress from bullying can create in the life of the sufferer is endless. Cancers can be attributed to bullying, as explained by Inna Segal, in her book, *The Secret Language of your Body*: "Feeling limited, carrying wounds from the past, attacking yourself from within, constant seeking approval, pleasing others, not able to let go of the past, etc."

When working with my clients, the saddest realisation for them during and after the Soul Journey Session to uncover the core belief memory, is that they could have prevented the ill health (cancer, tumours, blood pressure, heart disease, etc.) from forming or progressing, if they had known how to access and clear this negative core memory and belief.

By never being able to access and release the shutdown, humiliation, shame, guilt and other unresolved emotions of the past, the negative core belief continues to create the same experience and negative outcome in your present life, bringing about more pain, disease and negativity.

Numbness from feeling any emotion is another by-product of being the target of bullying. If you don't react, you're overlooked and left alone. Tears are a sign of weakness, which in turn becomes a game for the bully to 'play' with you like a toy, embarrass you in front of others or make you the joke for the group to taunt you. I learned to suppress the emotions and numb myself by creating pain; digging my fingernails into the palm of my hand, to take my mind off being the bully's target. This was my childhood and continued into my adult life because I never learned to switch it off.

You learn to suppress the emotions and numb out to stay away from the bully. People do this by taking drugs, alcohol and other addictions, but the unresolved emotion will come out in different ways. Just like a volcano erupts under pressure, the body will erupt under the pressure of unresolved emotions.

"What you resist always persists. Be willing to look within and release it."

It reminds me of the saying 'the straw that breaks the camel's back'. The 'straw' is not the present time in life, it's the original unresolved memory that has built up pressure over time to explode and be released. The body not being able to hold or take it anymore, explodes at the worst time and place possible, causing even more emotional trauma.

Most bully victims I see, as well as my own personal experience, swallow the abuse, become silent with self-inflicting negative self-talk. This is like the victim swallowing hand grenades and imploding. The person can become passive in nature (people pleasing, quiet achievers) or even become passive-aggressive. Then they are so sorry for what they did or said, feeling shame and guilt, swallowing the negative energy again. It's like they vomit the negative emotions that are their truth, then pick up the pieces and swallow them again, without realising the damage and the cycle repeating.

When I am psychically looking at a client's energy field, with this stored up negative energy, I tell them, "This energy could destroy or kill the wrong person."

It's better to go back into the past memory at the specific age with all the people present when this core belief was created and speak to the person responsible. We do this by imagination and visualisation techniques, using a teleporter, Tardis or time-machine, to travel back in time, to the original core memory and age.

We then can say all the things they never got to say, empty the negative emotions from the parts of their body which are still storing the unresolved conversations. Clearing it at the soul and cellular level, re-parenting, and replacing the negative with positive, loving and supportive resources allows the change to flow forward to all other times beyond that age, up to the present time; clearing, healing and bringing back balance.

LIFE REGRETS – WHAT IT COSTS YOU!

Did you know that holding onto past negative experiences and suppressing the emotions is the major cause of all health problems in the world today, suicide and cancer being the worst? Living with regret, guilt and shame is the biggest cause of people living unfulfilled, unhealthy lives which the take to their deathbeds.

You've heard the saying "It's not what you have done in your life, it's what you haven't done or said which you regret the most on your death bed."

What have you regretted not saying, doing, completing or becoming in your life so far? Anytime in your past, were you told:

- Get over it
- Don't tell anyone
- Time will heal all
- Toughen up
- You weren't good enough, pretty enough, clever enough, fast enough, etc.
- You get what you deserve
- You're not worthy of...
- You don't have the guts to...
- What will others think?
- You made your bed, now lie in it!
- Or you weren't heard when you said "No!"

These were all words you experienced several times for it become your current life truth. This memory became a belief about how the world should treat you, and then it became a vow in your mind that you must keep repeating until you learn the lesson or change the magnetic imprint of attraction. The memory could have been last week, last year, or in your childhood.

No matter what you do, learn or change as you get older, this past belief still haunts your mind, lives in your nervous system and you cannot stop it. Maybe you regret not saying what you needed to say before someone left or died? Lost something or someone without your control? Felt guilty or ashamed? Made a huge mistake in the past and are unable to forget? Cannot live up to others' expectations? Have been bullied or abused?

These and many more are issues clients have cleared within Soul Journey Sessions, giving them another chance to live life to their fullest.

What's your story? What are your repeating patterns, behaviours, habits, addictions? Who or what do you stand up for? What does your career say about you?

My story was attracting the same boss or friend who bullied me, never taking my side or respecting me; overruling, dominating, micro-managing, many times singling me out and picking on me. The friend or family member taking over off you, without asking, just assuming, you still had no voice.

One of my bosses who bullied me almost burst a vein in his neck when I finally stood up to him and refused what he was requesting me to do. It had taken a lot of guts for me to stand up and shout at him to stop bullying and harassing me to do things that weren't in my job description. That small moment toughened me up and taught me to defend myself and my role, even stronger.

WHAT BULLYING AND ABUSE DOES TO US

With my clients and my own story of being sexually abused at a young age, I have found the results are always the same. There is an "identity" or "stigma" of being bullied, being the abused victim. Abuse of any kind carries with it shame and guilt, locking the person into either shutting down or lashing out. They hold onto this negative core belief and it has repeated automatically, unconsciously, throughout their life. It's locked into their nervous system and until they release the 'charge' trigger or magnetic imprint of their belief, it continues on.

They keep attracting to them what they needed to experience to learn the lesson, release it, and move forward in life. The original negative core belief – *I'm not good enough, I'm not strong enough, I'm not lovable, I don't matter, I'm not worthy* – they've taken on at a young age is the same belief continuously attracting and repeating in their life.

> *"It's not what others think or say about us, the problem is what we keep repeating to ourselves."*

Their critical subconscious mind takes on the Core Belief and keeps repeating it internally, *"Look how ugly I am. OMG, I can't believe I said that! I did that? I'm so stupid, I'm so bad. No wonder no one loves me."*

These internal messages playing on a repeating loop keep us captive in this internal self-critical and judgemental web. What we say to ourselves internally we would never say to our kids, a friend, even our pet, but we continue to say these things to ourselves and believe it to be true.

We are meaner to ourselves than anyone else could be. We have become the bully to ourselves, we have disowned our younger self! The bullying that was endured in childhood becomes a blueprint for your current life. That memory is alive and causing your current problems. That is why you attract the same pattern, or personality repeatedly.

> *"The way you treat yourself sends a very clear message to others about how they should treat you."* - Denise Linn

This is our Inner Bully, Inner Critic, our own worst enemy, and we need to become friends with it. Where did it come from and how can we change the recording? We'll find out in a later chapter.

Once you learn this you can begin to understand that what you experience on the outside is a direct mirror of the deepest thoughts and beliefs you have about yourself, whether you remember or not. The negative personalities and outside experiences are your teachers, forcing you to look within, clear the memory and re-parent yourself. When you learn the lesson, the pattern, the spell breaks and you're free to move forward in your life.

It's like the invisible energy is written all over your face. Imagine playing that game called Celebrity Head, where you have a name of a celebrity on a headband, placed on your head. You don't know what the name is and can't see it, but other participants give you hints and you must guess who or what it is.

Instead of a celebrity name, you've got the negative belief energy stuck to your auric field, written all over your face.

You have the old belief invisibly written on your forehead for people to make you experience the feeling of what needs to change. If your belief is, 'I'm not good enough', you will attract people and experiences to make you feel not good enough. A relationship might start out well, but the end result will always be 'I'm not good enough'. They may even turn into your worst nightmare, with emotional turmoil fuelling your problems. Your mind-genie giving you proof, "You really aren't good enough, see I told you so."

Think about your life, what beliefs are you currently 'wearing' and attracting to you? Fact is, no one can make you feel anything you don't already have within your energy field. If you are being triggered, or your bruise being poked, look back on your life and see where it happened first, what or who does this remind you of?

The suppressed old belief with unresolved emotions stays in your body, in your energy fields, until you trace them back, face them, acknowledge them and then erase and replace them.

The problem is, your subconscious mind, the gatekeeper of your thoughts, won't allow you to release them easily. It actually believes you're "not good enough" (or whatever your belief may be). It believes what others said or did to you and won't release you from this eternal prison sentence, your mind-genie is in charge.

Emotional neglect can take many forms, from a parent having unrealistically high expectations or not listening attentively, to invalidating a child's emotional experiences to the point he or she begins to feel self-doubt. When a parent is not emotionally attuned to a child, there is no mirror held up, no positive reflection being shared with the child. Developing a positive sense of self, then, becomes more challenging for the child. Emotional neglect is generally unrecognised by the child until symptoms begin to appear in adulthood, by that stage the behaviour and personality are set.

Most people grow up believing there is something wrong with them. You then begin to search for the missing relationship in your life, looking for love in the wrong places, as they say. You need to learn to accept all parts of you that others chose not to, step away from their negative opinions, expectations their type of world.

Please note, it is never too late to start again. My clients and I are proof of this and you can follow the road I have paved, throughout this book and my website. Every day is a new day to start afresh. Our problem is not believing this to be true, but there is an end to this spell.

I believe in you and your soul believes in you. That's why you're here reading this book and haven't left this world by passing over. The universe needs you to step up and take your place with your soul purpose and passion again.

> "Your beliefs and thoughts are wired into your biology. They become your cells, tissues, and organs. There's no supplement, no diet, no medicine, and no exercise regimen that can compare with the power of your thoughts and beliefs. That's the very first place you need to look when anything goes wrong with your body." - Christiane Northrup, Goddesses Never Age: The Secret Prescription for Radiance, Vitality, and Well-Being

> "Your life will be transformed when you make peace with your shadow. The caterpillar will become a breathtakingly beautiful butterfly. You will no longer have to pretend to be someone you're not. You will no longer have to prove you're good enough. When you

embrace your shadow you will no longer have to life in fear. Find the gifts of your shadow and you will finally revel in all the glory of your true self. Then you will have the freedom to create the life you have always desired." - Debbie Ford

***

When I loved myself enough...

I began pouring my feelings into my journals, called surrender and gratitude. These loving companions speak my language, healed my soul and released the burden I had been holding onto.

***

***

When I loved myself enough...

I realised my mind-genie can torment and deceive me, keeping me in this game of life but I saw in the service of my heart it is a great and noble ally. I now know I can trust my mind genie to back me and my truth.

***

When I loved myself enough...

I forgave myself for all the times I thought I wasn't good enough, in the eyes and opinions of others. I learned to find my tribe where I was 'safe' to be and express who I am.

***

CHAPTER 5
SELF-COMPASSION AND SELF-LOVE RE-KINDLED
THE JOURNEY BACK TO SELF-HEALING, FROM THE INSIDE OUT

"Unresolved childhood trauma including abuse (complex trauma) affects 5 million Australian adults. Such trauma is associated with substantial physical and mental health challenges and psychosocial issues." - Blue Knot Services

We were all born whole and complete, loving and pure. Little by little, piece by piece, parts of us were replaced by the circumstances we were born into and people surrounding us. Negative patterns evolve for several reasons as I have mentioned in this book so far.

What's important is for us to stop and take notice of the lessons there are to learn to move forward.

A child growing up in an alcoholic, abusive environment may create a wall around themselves for protection. Such defensive methods may ensure surviving emotionally and physically through challenging and threatening times in their young life. Years pass, however, and though now safe, these walls and other defensive mechanisms are now invisible, yet still remain, sabotaging their personal and professional life.

The wall is no longer needed. It has become habitual behaviour. The first step is to become aware of what we have built around us. What stories our mind-genie continues to tell us to fortify the wall with fears.

As Rania Naim said:

"You can't find yourself among those who made you feel lost, abandoned and misunderstood. You can't revive your Soul when

you're surrounded by those who wrecked it. You can't love your voice when you're surrounded by the same people who told you that you don't have one. You can't rebuild yourself around those who destroyed you.

You can't use their bricks as a foundation because it won't hold you together. It never did. Sometimes we think that we can't change our environment or it's too late to find a new one, but it's never too late. It's never too late to realize that you don't deserve to live or work with people who bring you more misery than happiness and joy. Be it family, friends or others.

It's never too late to understand that you don't have to be punished every time you disagree with them. It's never too late to walk away from any environment that doesn't nourish your mind, body, heart and soul."

This chapter is the first step to your inner peace, freedom, balance, and harmony. Know that whatever negative experiences you've had so far can always be changed, deleted, and new seeds sown.

When you feel you cannot go on, the world is against you and you have years of repeated negative experiences to confirm your beliefs, I want you to start journaling your thoughts onto paper.

I want you to start today, right now, this will be your first step to compassionately loving your own Self back to life. We'll go into more detail on how to do this effectively in chapter 9 on Journaling. Don't ever give up hope!

Treat your ego mind as a genie. It is here to grant your personal wishes. Your mind-genie listens to your thoughts, and whichever has the loudest energy, whatever you think or speak about the most, wins and the mind-genie wants to please you and brings it true for you.

We are the creators of our everyday experiences, positive or negative. So, knowing your thoughts and beliefs have created your negative life experiences, you now know you can un-create and unbecome what you were taught or the perception you believed.

Your mind-genie seeks proof and makes the world match what we unconsciously expect or believe it to be, based on the original core memory we still hold onto.

Your mind-genie brings to your life the fears you don't like, the outcomes you don't want, the negative experiences you don't need. So how do you change it, how do you take back control? Learning to love and listen to your inner child is the first step.

You need to back yourself, get to know yourself again, and it starts with self-confession, self-compassion, journaling, connecting to your body and its needs.

Know thyself to heal thyself. The power of personal secrecy, self-honesty, begins with you. Only YOU need to know your inner truth, just you and your God source, your higher power, your soul.

Learn to listen to your intuition, your inner child's voice, which is quiet and subtle. Give it a voice and listening to what the message coming back is. As you are reading this book, note down what your life is like now. What you didn't receive as a child; when you grew up, what you gave that you never received, to your family, friends and loved ones.

As an adult, your mind-genie still won't allow you to receive it either. Your mind-genie has become the person who hurt you in the past. There will be unconscious resentment and jealousy, sometimes anger and unfairness felt internally, and that energy will ooze out into your thoughts and actions to others. We suppress these negative (called dark or shadow) emotions, so as not to offend or hurt other people's feelings – the opposite of how we were treated in the past.

In your journal write about what's going on in your life right now. Relationship problems? Career? Finances? Health? Then write down your default patterns, what do you do or fall back into when someone bullies, teases or abuses you? Do you fix, rescue, save or want to change others? Do you attract the same type of personalities to you? Are you saying one thing and receiving the opposite to your request from your God?

My defaults were being a frozen statue with any confrontation, then becoming self-critical to myself afterwards. A chameleon, blending into the group. An observer, to know what I needed to change into, which mask to wear, for acceptance, to fit in or belong. I wanted to make people feel good about themselves, helping them, which was draining my energy not filling it up. I know now this is an 'unhealthy empath behaviour'.

Be honest in your writing. What are you seeking in life? Maybe you're like me, in robot mode, not truly understanding what you're seeking. What are you addicted to wanting and searching for? Is it approval? Acceptance? Love? To belong?

Years after my soul awakening with Soul Coaching®, at my surprise fiftieth birthday, I realized I had been surrounded by my 'soul' mothers all my life. These were older females who treated me like a daughter or sister but were not my physical mother. I cried with joy and thanked them personally and in my prayers.

My mind-genie kept me in this spell, wanting my mother to open the door of her heart to me, while my soul had given the love and attention I needed through these soul mothers. Have a look around in your life and see if you have soul mothers or fathers who treat you like you were their child or sibling. Then give thanks to them and write about it in your gratitude journal.

In the past I had feared to feel negative emotions, anger, upset, rejection, abandonment and more. I had trained myself not to feel these throughout my life to survive and forgot to switch back on. I call it an 'emotional stroke' and like a physical stroke, I had to learn to feel again, to express all feelings fully and to release them from my body, mind and energy fields in a healthy way. Also, I had learned how, when, and where to feel safe to allow myself to do this.

Hundreds of my clients are the same. We had gathered all these negative experiences and traumatic blockages over our lives and kept them within us in the nervous system, instead of releasing, dissolving as we go. Think of a little baby, they laugh, giggle, hurt themselves and cry, finish and see something interesting, go and explore and the day goes on.

This is what we are meant to do – express the emotion fully, not stop it, store it, swallow it, and keep it within us. This was my problem. The 'stories' of my negative family life in childhood were being replayed automatically, unconsciously and on autopilot. I felt I was living with a split personality in my head, one side of self against the other, adult against inner child. I was fighting the outside world, believing the core belief to be true and defending, losing sleep and my mind-genie bringing my fears to life.

Fears are negative and surround the core belief, while wishes, dreams and goals are positive. If you have low self-worth and low self-esteem it is hard to hold onto anything positive. So, the fears win and become the wish you didn't want, the mind-genie delivering yet again, what you didn't want.

"Feelings are meant to be felt, all feelings negative and positive. When you allow yourself to acknowledge that feeling, anger, resentment, held from past memories, it no longer has the power over you." - Dr Christiane Northrup

Many of us used to say, "I don't want to turn out like my mother or father!" Then, when we have our own children, we speak like our parents and do exactly what we didn't want to do. It is because the thoughts and fears were louder in the mind than what we *did* want. The fears became the wish for the mind-genie to make true.

"What we are today comes from our thoughts and core beliefs of yesterday, and our present thoughts build our life of tomorrow: Our life is the creation of our mind." – Buddha

Your soul will bring the memory to be cleared to the surface, only when your body can handle it.

Remember, this is not about blaming others, it's about taking self-responsibility. Our parents did the best they could with what they had but they were also run by their subconscious little inner child's unresolved and unexpressed memories of their past. It's like a waterfall effect, with so many fears and beliefs handed down throughout the generations, cultures, and life without realizing the damage it causes if not cleared at the cellular level.

Stevan Thayer, Founder of Integrated Energy Therapy, says:

"Every cell in our body has the ability to remember. Our cellular memory can store the memory of: Physical, emotional and mental trauma. When trauma is suppressed into the cellular memory, the energy of that trauma can get stuck. The problem with suppressed cellular memory is not only does it limit our ability to live freely and joyfully in life, but it can also support the body in developing illness."

Looking back at how fortunate I was to be guided by my soul, to learn Soul Coaching®, the Journey Method™, Visionary Intuitive, Shamanic rights, Trauma Release and other modalities, I was then able to clear connections and anchors from the past to enable myself to be of the highest healing vibration possible, for me and also the ones I teach and heal.

It is not what happens to us, it is what we do to change those memories. Being able to turn from negative to positive and leading a healthy, wholesome life. It's not what's wrong with you, it's what happened to you that will unlock the vault of Pandora's box of past negative core belief memories.

Unconsciously I had already begun treating my children the negative way my parents had treated me, and I didn't like it. Because of my learnings, I was able to clear the negative DNA strands of energy and cellular memories, backwards for several generations plus forward to my children and grandchildren, releasing the burdens they would possibly carry, as I had done.

The more memories and core beliefs I have uncovered and unbecome, the more I see fragments of my innocent little self in my grandchildren. Soul is showing me what I would have been like if I hadn't taken on the beliefs and expectations of others, according to their 'rules of life'. It makes my heart sing each day I see my children and grandchildren.

> *"You can't fix a problem with the same consciousness or negative thinking that got you into that situation in the first place."*
> *- Albert Einstein*

When I first began a journey of healing by learning to rekindle and practice my own self-compassion and self-love, my body resisted. It didn't believe what my conscious mind and thoughts were speaking. It was as if I had been adopted and learned that negative way of living, but now the real loving soul family wanted me back, teaching me their new way of life. It took time and now I am able to easily say how blessed I am, loving and accepting all parts of me, thanking myself and mind-genie for the positive, loving gifts I am seeing and receiving. People on the outside respond to me the way I am treating myself, and it will happen to you too.

Being able to step outside of myself, see my world from a different point of view, I was able to see my parents and other 'soul teachers' who have come into my life through different eyes. I can now understand, learn the lesson and then forgive myself and others for the acting parts we all played in this game called 'life'.

When I complete any Soul Journey Core Belief session, the person/s who are connected within the memory either come closer in the relationship or are disconnected completely, whichever is for the highest and greatest good. I love when soul does this for me, all I need to do is trust. God and soul have never let me down, only my mind-genie has let me down for many years by not trusting.

Forgiveness does not mean 'what you did to me is ok'. It simply means you are no longer willing to carry around pain in response to someone's actions. Knowing this allowed me to heal easily, to forgive and release without guilt or shame from my past holding me back.

We have been living and experiencing the weeds of negativity, shame, guilt, fear, which were planted within our emotional and mental energy field, by the adult/s in our childhood. Now is the time to remove the old weeds at the root and plant new seeds, ones we choose and finally re-parent our own little self.

Plant the seeds of kindness, love, gentleness, hope, commencing today. Then watch your mind-genie bring to life those new seeds for you to harvest and enjoy in the days, months and years ahead.

"Deep within each of us is a longing for home. We yearn for a place of comfort where we can be ourselves, where we can realize our dreams." - Denise Linn

CHAPTER 6
STEPS TO SELF-LOVE AND SELF-COMPASSION

Let's start from here, where you are, right here and now, by stating, "This is not how my story is going to end!"

Self-Compassion = Self-Connection = Self-Love!

Find a photo of your younger self, about five years old, put this picture beside your bed or in your purse or wallet. You will be saying prayers and intentions to your younger version, morning and night. Setting up a daily routine and habit with consistency and timing.

Self-Compassion is the antidote to self-criticism and self-judgement. This combined daily with self-love is a magical gift to self and can bring your life back to health and happiness, within a small-time period. It will help you fill up the depleted cellular memories caused by loneliness, sadness, grief, and hardship to overflowing with love, connectedness and joy.

How do you talk to yourself? Lovingly, supportive or judgemental and critical? Most times you're speaking to yourself the way your mother, father or other significant person spoke to you as a child. Now you need to delete it and install your own positive, encouraging self-talk.

Once you are aware of your inner critical voice, next time you catch yourself saying something nasty to yourself, pause, and say, "delete, delete, delete." This sends a message to your subconscious mind to ignore what you just thought. Now install it with what you choose and state, "install, install, install."

So, to help you change the tone of your inner voice, imagine yourself as the child in the photo. Tuning into that younger inner child allows you to look at yourself without judgement. If it's too hard, how would you talk to your friend's child or your pet? They just want to be loved and heard. Ask questions like, "What do you really want to do now? Have now? Eat now?" Then do this for yourself.

SELF-LOVE AND SELF-GIVING
True love in an unconditional feeling of appreciation, acknowledgement and acceptance for your-Self. Unconditional means that no matter what you do, you will always love yourself with the same strength. This IS Self-Love.

You need to learn how to give yourself whatever you're giving to others, treating yourself equally. Take the advice you give to others, as it is the best advice you ever will get. Catch yourself giving the advice to friends, family or others and acknowledge how wise you have become from your lessons in the past, then implement that advice for you.

"One of the biggest lessons I learned from nearly dying of cancer is the importance of loving myself unconditionally. In fact, learning to love and accept myself unconditionally is what healed me and brought me back from the brink of death." - Anita Moorjani

TEACHING OTHERS
We need to teach others how we want to be treated. We do this by first changing the negative core belief memory and emotions. Treat yourself how you would like a friend to treat you, a lover, your money. You need to do this for you, being kind and gentle, praising an encouraging of yourself. Buy or do something that you would love to have as a reward or celebration of this new stage of loving yourself. When you love yourself, honour your word, respect yourself, accept all aspects of yourself, others WILL treat you the same. *Monkey see, monkey do.*

BOUNDARIES

People treated you the way you felt about yourself back in the unresolved memory. Write down what you will no longer tolerate in your life, what you will accept, how you want to be treated. This will start putting in place boundaries for you.

Review your life and understand how in the past your unhealthy empath behaviour has given away your power and energy to vampires (people who drain your life force energy, consciously or unconsciously). Recognise the patterns and have a confident 'No' for them. Also have consequences if they do step over your line.

By sealing up the energy leaks you will have more opportunities open for you to follow your soul path and purpose in life. Your vibration, love, and light will increase, attracting and allowing like-minded beings to come into your life.

Realising I was an 'Empath introvert' personality allowed me to accept myself easier. I could see where others would take advantage of my nature and where I needed to be more confident in saying 'No', before getting hooked into compassion fatigue and not getting out.

Empaths are needed spiritually in life. Learn to understand more about your empath nature and protect this gift you have. Respect and build your boundaries so you can share your gift and light where it's needed the most.

SELF-HONESTY

Write down your default patterns, the ones you have learned and followed all your life under the old programming. When you're not conscious in daily living you can fall back into the old habits or behaviours.

It's ok, forgive yourself. As the Japanese proverb says, 'Fall down seven times and stand up eight'.

This builds self-acceptance and you can keep what serves you and release the patterns that drain you. Self-awareness gives you permission to release the patterns, habits and behaviours which controlled you in the past. It gives you the choice to move forward into freedom. Sometimes people don't want to change, they prefer to stay in the situation you are in. Either way, it's still your choice.

Some of my default programming from a negative neglected childhood were:

- It's my fault this happened
- I'm responsible to make it right or responsible for others
- I must make up for this
- Making excuses for other people
- They, parents, siblings, want me to fail
- I say the wrong thing to people to set them off
- Convincing the sceptics, forgetting the supportive ones
- Seeking attention, good or bad, is attention
- Its ok not be paid, just to please, keep them quiet or give away
- Constant need to be important/wanted/needed
- I'm going to do anything to make ……proud/happy
- Resistance to change, when it's the right soul change.
- Take no action towards your goals
- Burnout/Compassion Fatigue
- Silent, shy, don't take risks
- Avoid confrontation at all costs, give in to others and settle for less than others
- Can't switch off, still plugged into childhood beliefs, not able to delegate or ask for help in current life
- Be the people pleaser against your body intuition
- Give until it hurts
- Being an empath

Now make your own list and add to it in the days and weeks ahead. You are getting to know your-Self, which is the first important step to healing your-Self.

SELF-RESPONSIBILITY

You are only ever responsible for your part, your share of anything. Don't be conned into believing anything different. While still holding onto past negative core belief memories, you can automatically assume responsibility for other people's actions throughout your life. It's a childhood consequence of the memory which needs to be disconnected. Allowing you to be free and allowing the karmic energy to flow back to the other people involved.

Compassion fatigue can be the result of being attached to the negative childhood memories. Not able to stop saving, rescuing, fixing others, people or animals, no matter how many you have already helped.

The following statements, if true for you, may carry forward as wounds into adulthood. Tick whichever ones apply to you or write them in your Journal. Releasing and them letting go will allow greater healing to happen for you.

Close your eyes after reading the statement, connect with the feeling your body gives you, is it true or false, reaction or stillness?

- I wasn't allowed to make my own decisions, even when I was old enough to
- A parent confided in me or expected me to take care of him or her
- One of my parents abandoned me, emotionally or physically
- One of my parents flew into rages
- As a child, I had to endure sexual attention or abuse
- The way I was treated as a child made me feel unlovable
- I was criticized harshly as a child
- My parents made me feel guilty for being my true self

- I was neglected as a child
- My parents didn't see or appreciate me for who I really am
- A parent made me endure physical closeness that I didn't want
- As a child, I was judged in ways that made me feel ashamed
- As a child, I was blamed for things that others did
- My parents expected me to perform to make them feel good about themselves
- Though my physical needs were taken care of as a child, I wasn't cared for or loved
- I was supposed to do what a parent wanted, not what I wanted
- As a child, I wasn't forgiven when I did something wrong
- As a child, I was publicly exposed in embarrassing ways
- As a child, I was treated in a way that made me feel that I shouldn't exist
- I trusted one of my parents and then he or she turned on me
- I witnessed violence as a child
- A parent was absent emotionally or indifferent to me
- As a child, my body boundaries were intruded on
- As a child, my peers rejected or ignored me
- My parents focused on my externals or achievements and ignored my true self
- As a child, I wasn't given enough nurturing, touch, or feeding
- My family made me feel bad for violating their morals
- My family acted like they didn't particularly like me
- A parent used my confidential thoughts or writings against me
- A parent compared me negatively to my siblings or peers

With gratitude to https://www.blueknot.org.au

I had only three statements of the above list not ticked. I fitted the bill. When ticking these statements, yes or no, it came as a relief for me to know what I and my clients are displaying in adulthood can always be traced back to childhood, even though some could not remember. It inspires hope for change and a healed future. The mind-genie doesn't want you to be in pain, so it will keep it hidden.

If you resonated with any of the above statements and are ready for change, [go here for a for a free 20-minute Healing Assessment with me - http://bit.ly/2u7vf1j](http://bit.ly/2u7vf1j)

> *"Hurt people, hurt people. Healed people change the world, by changing themselves first."*

PHYSICALLY LOVING YOURSELF

When you walk past your reflection in the mirror, say something nice instead of criticism. Put your hand on your upper chest and tell your inner child, your body, "You are safe, I am here for you."

After a time, your body will relax when you do this. It feels like someone strong putting their hand on your shoulder and telling you, "It will be okay, you are safe now, I've got you", only this is you to your inner child.

Look at yourself in the mirror, look into your own eyes, visualise yourself as a little five-year-old and say, "I love you, I love you, I love you."

EXERCISING

When you exercise it helps express and release negative stored emotions from your body. Exercising in nature is even better as nature connects you back to life force and the universe.

Train yourself to see something new each day and be grateful for it. Giving thanks to God, Buddha, whichever you resonate with, by connecting to your highest power. Soul can guide, provide, care for you, listen and return to you what you most desire. Connect with soul and ask, "If this is what you want me to do, show me the way, I surrender, thank you." Then have faith and trust that this or something better is coming into your life soon.

YOUNG LIVING ESSENTIAL OILS

Use the Young Living Essential Oils regime in Chapter 7. Your body will respond to the smells of the oils as well as putting them onto your body, massaging the oils in, connecting through touch and stimulating your senses.

I imagine I am anointing myself with the luxury of oils, massaging with love for myself, thanking each part of my body. Many of the Young Living essential oils are certified to be taken internally and used in cooking. I also take their supplements filled with essential oils, I use the cleaning products, personal products and makeup, allowing my body and living quarters a chemical-free space to heal and grow. We'll look at essential oils in more depth in a later chapter, but for more information, go to http://bit.ly/2u5xOkx

EATING

Watch what you are eating. Make a promise to feed yourself healthy food, enough food, not an excess of food. Observe if you're shoving food and or alcohol in, drowning yourself. Journal your thoughts and who makes you feel like this. Express your truth in other ways; your body doesn't deserve to be treated this way, as a dumping vessel.

DRINKING

Drink pure, filtered water which cleanses the toxins, acids and negative emotions from your body. The body organs need water to help hydrate and function at the optimum level. Negative emotions cause acidity and imbalance in the body. Put essential oils into tap water.

I realised when I wasn't coping with work, I turned to alcohol. This was only allowing me to relax and to drown my sorrows, never releasing them. I am fortunate I learned a new way to release and renew.

LOVE, LOVE, LOVE

Choose love – love of self and then love for others. Find pictures, words and ornaments of love and place them around your living spaces, bedroom, and office. Let your eyes see these love symbols, allowing the mind and body to absorb the love you have for yourself.

Listen to love songs and imagine singing them to your inner child. Notice who comes into your life after completing these exercises, acknowledge the compliments, the gifts coming your way. Write about them in your gratitude journal, remembering to write at least five things every day you are grateful and happy for. This will program your mind-genie to find even more for you to enjoy.

L – Love

O – Overcomes

V – Victimhood and

E – Emotional neglect

***

When I loved myself enough...

I learned to grieve for the hurts in life when they happen instead of making my heart heavy from lugging them around to deal with later on

***

When I loved myself enough...

I quit trying to be a saviour and rescuer for others. Accept them as they are and change my internal thoughts about myself!

***

CHAPTER 7
ESSENTIAL OILS TO LIVE AGAIN BY YOUNG LIVING
RECONNECTION TO SELF THROUGH SMELL, TASTE AND TOUCH

I first learned about Essential oils when I attended a Mind, Body, Spirit festival. I purchased a bottle of Valor for my stress and anxiety caused by bullying and intimidation in the workplace. The Young Living Essential Oils distributor said the blend was used in the Roman days for the soldiers going to war to give them strength and courage.

I could sure use a lot of that.

This is how my journey with Young Living began. Since then, the Essential Oils and supplements have helped heal many other health challenges I once faced.

I have loved reading the history behind the Young Living brand, by the founder, Dr Gary Young. He has researched biblical times and whatever healed the body in those times he has brought forward to the present day to help balance and enhance people's lives in ways I never knew possible.

Soul led me to the brand, Young Living, as I was using other types to no avail for my health. Since that day, Young Living has been a huge factor in overcoming the bullying, abuse and other emotional issues I thought I could never be released from.

In this chapter, I'm going to talk about their Feelings Kit, which contains six blends of oils designed to connect and enhance the relationship with your body and bring about balance to all parts of your life, emotionally, physically, mentally, and spiritually.

The Inner Child blend alone contains Orange, Tangerine, Jasmine, Ylang-Ylang, Spruce, Sandalwood, Lemongrass, and Neroli. When we become disconnected from our inner child or identity it causes confusion. The Inner Child blend helps us reconnect to ourselves.

Because I had held onto these memories for so long, I needed an added way to release the grip the emotional stroke had over my body. My mind said one thing while my body gave me a different response with so many health problems. The Feelings Kit came at the right time for me.

Natural essential oils are the lifeblood of a plant. They protect the plant from disease, provide nutrients and help fight off anything it doesn't want. It keeps the plant (or tree, fruit, bark, root, etc.) healthy and functioning at its best.

Young Living's essential oils can do the following:

- Reach every cell in your body within 20 minutes when applied topically to the body
- Support the natural detoxification process in your body
- Help support your body's natural regeneration process
- Have the capability of passing the "blood-brain" barrier
- Work on emotions via the limbic system of your brain when inhaled
- Help to release emotional trauma, relax and clear the mind
- Help to transport nutrients to starving human cells
- Act as powerful antioxidants
- Increase atmospheric oxygen
- Help purify the air
- Increase ozone and negative ions in the area it is diffused, creating a cleaner atmosphere.

Just by breathing in Young Living essential oils it affects every single cell in your body within 20 minutes. They quickly work on your amygdala (when you think of the amygdala, you should think of one word. *Fear*). The amygdala is the reason we're afraid of things outside of our control. It also controls the way we react to something we see as potentially threatening or dangerous. This is in the Limbic system of your brain, behind your forehead.

Look at - http://bit.ly/2u5xOkx to get your Oils Discovery eBook.

When it comes to using oils for your emotional health (which is really your overall health because 87-93% of disease comes from our thoughts and emotions) what should we look for? I researched different companies with essential oils and Young Living were the right fit for healing my health, my family and those of my clients.

When you begin a daily routine with the oils, you are honouring and respecting your body, connecting to the universal energy of chakras with healing taking place on many levels.

VALOR II

Valor II is the first blend to use when preparing for an emotional release. It helps balance the energies within the body and gives courage, confidence, and higher self-esteem. Valor balances and equalizes the body's energies thereby increasing oxygen intake to the pineal gland (the seat of our higher intelligence and intuitive faculties). I use Valor whenever I need some courage to face challenges in my life.

Apply by massaging in 3-6 drops on each foot and the top of your shoulders. Cup your hands and breathe in the strength-giving aroma as it balances the body. You can also apply to feet at night time.

Affirmation: "I am ready to transform my life"

HARMONY

Harmony brings about a harmonic balance to the chakras (energy centres), allowing the energy to flow more efficiently through the body. It may reduce stress and create a general feeling of wellbeing. I was certainly out of balance within myself, as I lived in my head rather than my body. Whenever I am feeling out of sorts, I reach for the Harmony bottle.

Apply 1 drop of Harmony either directly on the energy centres (chakras) or along the side of the body, then breathe in the smell.

Affirmation: "I can express myself safely and completely"

FORGIVENESS

Forgiveness may help you move past the barriers in life. It also helps to bring a person into a higher spiritual awareness of their needs and helps raise their frequency to the point where they feel almost compelled to forgive, forget, let go, and go on with their lives.

Self-forgiveness is the hardest and last one to do if you've been self-critical and judgmental of self or others.

Apply 1 drop of Forgiveness around the navel in a clockwise motion (clockwise activates and connects to the auric field). Breathe in the smell.

Affirmation: "I forgive myself for my past mistakes"

PRESENT TIME

Present Time helps bring you into the moment. We must heal the past and stop worrying about the future. We must live in the moment and feel what is presently here to heal. When we're in our head, for survival purposes from our past, we are not present. This was me!

Apply 1 drop of Present Time behind the ears and 1 drop on the thymus (the gland just under your sternum) in a circular motion; then close your eyes and tap the thymus 3 times with the energy fingers (pointer and middle). Breathe in the smell too.

Affirmation: "I experience the joy of the present"

RELEASE

Release helps to enhance the release of stored memory trauma from the cells of the liver, where anger and hate emotions are stored. It may also help you let go of negative emotions so that progress is more effective and efficient. Release does exactly what it says it will – release.

Apply one drop of Release over the front and back of your liver in a circular motion. Again, breathe in the smell.

Affirmation: "I release all negativity from my body"

INNER CHILD

Inner Child may stimulate memory response and help you reconnect with your inner-self. This is one of the first steps to achieving emotional balance.

"When you are a child all things are possible. There are no limitations," says Gary Young, *"When you find your inner child, you have found your true self. The child in you is your creativity."*

Apply 1 drop of Inner Child under the nose and breathe in the smell.

Affirmation: "I am ready to face and release my inner child"

THE FEELINGS PROTOCOL

- Step 1: Apply Valor on the bottoms of your feet to balance your feelings.
- Step 2: Apply Harmony on the energy points of the body to release unpleasant energies.
- Step 3: Apply Forgiveness clockwise on the navel to let go of negative emotion.
- Step 4: Apply Present Time to the wrists and behind your ears.
- Step 5: Apply Release over the front and back liver in the circular motion.
- Step 6: Apply Inner Child under your nose.
- Step 7: Apply Valor once again to complete the Feelings Kit experience.

It's been said that when there's conflict between reason and feeling, human beings will always side with feeling. According to Gary Young, founder of Young Living, *"99% of life's decisions are made from feelings."*

Therefore, if you want your life to be guided by good decisions that lead to health, happiness, and fulfilment, you need to be aware of and in control of your present feelings and learn how to release the repressed emotions of the past.

Most of our feelings are not responses to current happenings. They originate from the programming in our cellular memory that was imprinted by the emotional experiences of our past that we were unable to understand, process, and resolve at the time.

These forgotten traumatic experiences function as live programming in our bodies, affecting every aspect of our lives and particularly in how we make decisions. When our thoughts are limited by fears, lack of self-worth, and not feeling good enough for more or better, we make decisions that limit our success. Limited thinking leads to limited decisions that lead to a limited life that falls short of the higher being-given potential we possess.

By focusing on fixing your feelings, you can help support feelings of balance in most aspects of your life – physical, mental, and spiritual. Essential oils are perfect vehicles to help you in this task because their molecules pass directly to the emotional brain and can bring us into contact with the issues we have long forgotten and enable us to deal with them and resolve them once and for all. When we clear our emotional baggage, we clear the way to manifest our true and highest potential.

According to Gary Young:

"Thought equals frequency. Essential oils absorb our thoughts. They are registered in the oils as intent. Intent is directed energy. When you apply an intent-energized oil on your feet they can saturate all

your cells within 60 seconds, stimulating creative thinking and pushing negative energy out of the cells, thus increasing the frequencies of the cells throughout the body. In that uplifted state you can create a new desire to be better tomorrow. You have no limitations but those you choose to accept."

He goes on to say:

"Use the Feelings Kit. Apply feeling oils before work and every night before bed. Do this for 30 days and you will change your life. You will feel enthusiastic. Your life will be full of excitement. And people will be drawn to you like a magnet."

It's also good to journal your thoughts and changes you experience along the way. Remember, you are reprogramming your mind which doesn't believe you can change. When you journal, your eyes will read the changes and only then your mind will believe it to be true. *Your heart sees it when it believes, your head believes only when it sees.*

Download your free Essential Oils Discovery eBook at
http://bit.ly/2u5xOkx

"Fear keeps us rooted in the past. Fear of the unknown, fear of abandonment, fear of rejection, fear of not having enough, fear of not being enough, fear of the future-all these fears and more keep us trapped, repeating the same old patterns and making the same choices over and over again. Fear prevents us from moving outside the comfort-or even the familiar discomfort-of what we know. It's nearly impossible to achieve our highest vision for our lives as long as we are being guided by our fears." - Debbie Ford

***

When I loved myself enough...

I found, If I love someone or something to set it free. If they come back they're yours, if they don't they never were.
Richard Bach

***

When I loved myself enough...

It was the hardest thing I've had to do and now it is so easy. It's now my daily ritual.

***

CHAPTER 8
CHAKRAS – UNIVERSAL LIFE FORCE CENTRES

The chakra (the Sanskrit word for wheel) are the energy centres or vortex in your aura that govern and regulate the energy entering and flowing throughout the physical and energy bodies. They are energy structures not physical organs.

The chakras are aligned along the central channel which runs along the spinal cord. Energies move up and down and in a spiral in and out along this channel and side channels.

Imagine an invisible rod through the top of your head (crown chakra), all the way down through the centre of your body – this is the internal cylinder for the chakras.

Chakras are composed of high-frequency energy strands that the spiritual eye perceives as light. The life force is channelled to the physical body and its organs via the meridians and enters the body through the chakras.

The degree of chakra activity depends on a combination of the physical, emotional, mental, and spiritual development of the individual. Chakras can be damaged or blocked through an emotional upset such as conflict, loss or accident. Fear, anxiety, and stress are also common causes of chakra malfunction. It's the disruption of the chakra and aura that create disease and disturb the energy balance of the chakras.

Psychological problems may cause 'blockages', obstructing the flow of energy into or out of the chakras. In general, the front aspects of the chakras correlate to our *emotional* function, the back to our *will* function, and the top three chakras to our *reason* function.

Balance in our reason, will, and emotion centres is vital for good health and wellbeing. The amount of energy flowing through our chakras determines how well we function. To connect to my soul and purpose, through the modality of Reiki, I needed to understand the universal life force centres of the Chakras; how my energy fields, if blocked, can stop the flow of this vital chi (life force).

To help you remember the chakra colours, think about a rainbow in the sky. Think about how amazingly God and Mother Nature has created these for us and more importantly what emotion blocks them. By understanding the blocks, you can access the memory that is required to clear and release for you to move forward in life again.

Connecting us to the web of life, physical, emotional, spiritual, and mental chakras, are a way to connect to the universal life force energy.

Root Chakra, Kundalini, Survival
Located: at the tailbone, base of the spine
Colours: RED, black

Element: earth, sense: smell

Governs: Physical awareness, vigour, heredity, survival, security, passion, feet, legs survival, trust, your relationship with money, home, and job.

Blocked by Fear!

Sacral Chakra, Sensation
Located: at sex organs or near belly button

Colour: ORANGE, brown

Element: water, sense: taste

Governs: Social awareness, sexuality, creativity, emotions, anger, fear, instinct to nurture, spleen, perceptions concerning food or sex.

Blocked by Guilt!

Solar Plexus Chakra, Power
Located: between the sternum bone and the belly

Colour: YELLOW

Element: fire

Sense: sight

Governs: Intellectual awareness, power, accomplishments, will, ego projections, vital energies, control, your freedom to be yourself.

Blocked by Shame!

Heart Chakra, Heart, Love
Located: at heart centre of chest

Colour: GREEN, pink

Element: air

Sense: touch

Governs: Emotional and Security awareness, love, compassion, mediates between higher and lower planes of being, healing, lungs breath prana, sense of time, relationships in your life. *Blocked by Grief!*

Throat Chakra, Creative
Located: at base of throat

Colour: SKY BLUE

Element: ether

Sense: hearing

Governs: Conceptual Awareness and Ideas, speech, hearing, communication, and self-expression.

Blocked by Lies!

Brow Chakra, Intuitive
Located: in centre of forehead above eyes
Colour: INDIGO

Element: spiritual vision

Sense: telepathy
Governs: Intuitive Awareness, intuition, thought, inner and outer sight, visions, dreams. *Blocked by Illusion!*

Crown Chakra, Spirit
Located: at top of head
Colour: VIOLET, white

Element: cosmic kingdom
Governs: Imaginative awareness, connection to cosmic consciousness, spiritual, wisdom aspirations knowledge of truth.

Blocked by Earthly attachments!

Palm, Finger and feet Chakras
The chakras in the palms of the hands are often relegated to minor status. But they are of great value in daily life and must be open and active for sharing Reiki treatments and other healing energies.

These chakras transmit healing energy and receive energetic information from the universe. The palm chakras are used to channel healing energies to yourself and others and to receive impressions of the energy of a room, person, situation, etc.

These chakras make a major difference in the quality of life when they can be opened by intention. Practice in becoming aware of the energy of the palm chakras is essential if you are at all interested in energy work and spiritual healing. Healing chakras also activate in the fingertips.

Feet chakras help channel energy up and down through Mother Earth and to ground oneself from negativity or excess energy.

Whenever I felt blocked, I would simply put my hand chakras on the part of the body for the chakra I needed. I would say 'Divine Healing Intelligence, please release what is no longer necessary in this chakra, imagining cleaning out residue, dust, etc and send it to an imagined purple flame for transmutation.

Keep moving from feet chakras, hand chakras, base, sacral, solar plexus, heart, throat, third eye, up to the crown chakra. Breathing it all out. Then asking your god source or soul to pour in a liquid of peace, unconditional love, abundance, freedom and whatever else you choose for you. Commencing pouring into the feet chakras, hand chakra and continue upwards.

***

When I loved myself enough...

I lost my fear of speaking my truth, for I have come to see how good it truly is.

***

***

When I began to love myself...

I started sharing about my life and views because I knew this was my right and my responsibility.

***

When I began to love myself...

I began to accept the unacceptable and I thrived on the new energy filling my world, led by Soul.

***

CHAPTER 9
JOURNALLING BACK TO YOUR SOULFUL LIFE
SURRENDER, GRATITUDE, WRITE & BURN/SHRED JOURNALING

Journaling is an expression of emotions, acknowledgement and acceptance in written form. It helps you rewire and reprogram your negative mindset to recreate your future direction, one piece and one day at a time.

When you're trying to heal from a conscious level— repeating affirmations and telling yourself you're healthy—there will be an invisible subconscious program that's sabotaging you. This article will give a more in-depth explanation - http://bit.ly.

Firstly, buy separate journals, one for 'surrender' and another for 'gratitude' or you can combine these into one book. Decorate it and make it special for you. Take your time and even ask your inner child how they would like it to look. Surrender and gratitude writing has a profound effect on clearing out emotional junk and clutter to make room for the abundance that's here and available for us.

If you want to use one book, this is the way to set out:

Surrender writing is written on the left-hand side of the page. Release by expressing the memories, hardships and emotions in your life, making space for the divine soul to replace.

Gratitude writing is on the right-hand side of the page. It connects you to expressing what you see, and being thankful for what you receive from soul.

Write the entries with the day's date and have a space in between so that you can go back at any time and see the changes which happen over time. When you surrender something, it will come back to you in a better form than you would have ever imagined.

You can keep the journal right next to your bedside. First thing when you wake in the morning, write in your surrender journal, last thing before you go to sleep at night, write five things you are grateful for, you like or makes you smile. Some people even create a digital journal. It's up to you, just get it done, however you choose.

Working with soul and the divine universe, your god source, is about manners. You ask with a polite request, release with faith, trusting you will receive what is rightfully yours, then give thanks when you receive it.

Surrender is releasing and letting go. There are times in life when you need to hold on, there are also times to let go and surrender. When I talk about surrendering, you are not surrendering to someone or something outside yourself, you are surrendering to the spirit within you. You are surrendering to your higher self, your higher wisdom. Letting go, trusting your higher self to take care of it.

What to write about in your surrender journal:

- Anything you are struggling with
- Anything that gives you anxiety, depression or negative feelings.
- Any relationships it may be time to let go of.
- Problems or situations that are out of your control, which don't serve you or support you anymore.

When you write this out in your Surrender journal and let go, handing the control over to your highest power, your needs will be met above and beyond your greatest expectations.

The Surrender Journal is not for the deepest negative emotions of anger, resentment, etc. Those are for the write and burn/shred journaling which we will discuss later. Remembering my teenage years when I was punished for writing my truth in my secret diary, I have learned it is important to dissolve the papers, offering it to your god, allowing karma to be released.

You need to trust and have faith it will fall into place for you. It does take practice. If you have been suffering for a long time, I am telling you from the experience of myself and the clients I teach, it is worth the wait.

Gratitude is a positive emotion, it's how you feel when you're thankful for something. A gratitude journal is a process of writing down what you're grateful for during the day. Sometimes this is the hardest thing to write about, especially if you've had a long list of negative experiences. But again, I'm telling you from my own experience it does work.

When you have gratitude in your life you:

- Feel grateful and it changes your perspective on the life that you've been given.
- Feel less victimized by others or by life. Blame no longer exists. Rather than looking at what you lost or what you don't have, you're able to reframe situations and move forward focusing on what you can do and what you do have.
- Have a more open heart. Gratitude helps you become more compassionate and empathetic to your own needs. You'll be able to connect with people even if you don't think you have much in common with them.
- Have a glass half full approach. With gratitude you'll be able to recognise and appreciate what you have rather than what you don't. As you begin to become aware of what is good and positive in your life, what is good and positive will grow.
- Reprogram your Reticulated Activating System (RAS), which will begin searching for what you want to see, rather than what you don't want to or fear to see. Your inner child, soul,

then creates more of what makes your heart sing, connecting you back to your Soul's life force energy.

Begin with writing five things you are grateful for at the end of each day. It can be small like your pet's unconditional love or it can be larger like the roof over your head, your job, your family or your life as a whole.

WRITE AND BURN/SHRED

The third part of Journaling is Write and Burn/Shred. This is the one which has helped me the most to energetically release the stored-up negative emotions. Emotions are supposed to be in motion, not stored and held onto.

Knowing that energy is like a boomerang and returns to you, whatever energy you send to another, you WILL receive back tenfold. Make sure what you think and speak are a positive intent. Release any negative emotions like anger, jealousy, revenge, resentment, into this Write and Burn/Shred part of journaling.

Remembering back to my teenage years when I sought refuge by writing my true feelings and thoughts at that stage in my life into my lockable diary, I can still feel the energy of being criticised and punished for what I had written privately. The nervous system holds onto the negative energy for as long as it takes for you to find and release it. By writing, then burning or shredding, it releases it more quickly from your system.

I also wrote a letter to my family, which I was again punished for, about how I was feeling at that time. It's easier to express onto paper as if you were talking to the person in front of you. Then burn or shred it. BUT NEVER SEND IT! I learnt the hardest way, see the case study.

To begin this process, lock the door, for privacy, and allow yourself time to write and express your unresolved emotions onto paper. You need lots of writing paper for this, a drink of water and willingness to let this go. Think of a negative memory which you cannot get out of your mind and you're unable to change.

Imagine yourself in this memory, who else is there? What age are you? Where are you feeling it in your body (this connects you back to your younger body). What do you need to say and to whom? You are connecting to yourself, back at a different time, observing from a distance, like you're watching a DVD of the memory.

Feel the emotion, whatever it may be – anger, jealousy, fear, sadness, resentment. When you are ready, open your eyes and write down whatever thoughts are coming through. DO NOT READ IT! This is most important as your mind-genie will want to criticize and judge your words, to keep you in a self-sabotaging role and you'll give up.

Your inner child finally has the courage to speak the truth only to be criticised and judged again, not feeling safe and remembering the past, the inner child will shut down and never express it again.

Just write and let out the emotions, express through crying, or however it needs to come out.

When you feel there is no more to write, close your eyes and connect back to the memory. Asking yourself in that memory, "What else needs to be said?" Again, feel where it is stored in your body, open your eyes and begin to write more, if needed.

When there are no more thoughts to write, rip the paper up, burn it or shred it, so nothing is left. You have just handed it back to the Creator of all things, your God, for karma to take place.

Wikipedia describes Karma as the following:

"Karma is the universal principle of cause and effect. Our actions, both good and bad, come back to us in the future, helping us to learn from life's lessons and become better people.

Karma is basically energy. Karma is the best teacher, forcing people to face the consequences of their actions and thus improve and refine their behaviour, or suffer if they do not. Even harsh karma, when faced with wisdom, can be the greatest spark for spiritual growth."

When we hold onto old memories, hoping something will change, we are holding onto the karma of the other person as well. It's best to access the memory and release it at the soul and cellular level for everyone to be set free.

When you're finished with your writing, place your hands on that same part of your body and with unconditional love flowing through your hand chakra's (centre of your palms), allowing the love from your heart and soul to flow into your body. Sending in love and healing with new seeds of peace, courage, confidence and whatever else you choose for yourself.

"The mind says, 'I'll believe it when I see it', the heart says, 'I'll see it when I believe it', listen more to your heart or your head will destroy you."

Trust and have faith in the divine spiritual energy that takes away our fears and core beliefs, hears our prayers and intentions and sends back to us what is rightfully ours, on a soul level. When you see and feel new changes and gifts appearing in your life, write it in your gratitude journal. Then place your hand on your upper chest and say, 'thank you' or 'Len-So-Mei' (Reiki energy meaning of pure unconditional love). This is another form of Self-Love connection through touch to your own inner child and your body.

Some additional questions for you to answer in your Write & Burn journal are:

- I'm angry at you because…… and that makes me feel……
- I'm scared because……
- I ……your behaviour because……
- I'm ashamed because……
- I feel disappointed because……

- You ruined my...... because......
- I'm afraid because......
- I'm embarrassed because......
- I feel really hurt because......
- You taught me to......
- The lesson I needed to learn here from you is...... (This one can also be written into your gratitude journal)
- If I could create something new for myself and life I wish...... (This one can also be written into your surrender journal)

CASE STUDY: CONTROLLED AND CONSTRICTED CLIENT

I had a client, Clare, sixty-three years old, who was completing the Journaling section for her session aftercare. She had become extremely agitated, not able to sleep through the night and called for help. We went through the whole process and she understood what needed to be done, all questions answered, and she started the process again. Within four days, Clare called again, very distraught and wanting to give up.

Going deeper into the process she had followed, I uncovered instead of keeping private and burn or shred the writings, her controlling husband was reading it and causing more arguments because of what Clare had honestly written. It was his critical feedback about her self-honesty which was causing the agitation and lack of sleep.

Within six months she had left her husband, finally being able to release herself from his controlling and constrictive behaviour of many years.

This shows you the power of Core Belief clearing sessions combined with Journaling and the steps to Self-love and Self-compassion.

"Soul always has a way of showing to us how far we have come; takes us full circle, for us to see and acknowledge our journey

ourselves. Listening to the whispers of your soul is just the beginning of your new life."

***

When I began to love myself...

I hugged my little self-everyday as many times as

I could and she loved that!

***

CHAPTER 10
HO'OPONOPONO PRAYER
TO MAKE IT RIGHT WITHIN, SPIRITUAL, SOUL WORK

Of the many prayers I have used over my life, this prayer is a miracle maker, especially when said to your own Inner Child. It is an ancient Hawaiian system called Ho'oponopono, which means 'To Make Right'. It changes your inner belief system and takes you to a higher level of energy vibration that moves you toward success in any area of life. It has changed my life and the lives of clients, family and friends around me.

I heard the story about a therapist in Hawaii who cured a complete ward of mentally ill patients without ever seeing any of them. The psychologist would study an inmate's chart and then look within himself to see how he created that person's illness. As he cleared and improved himself, the patient improved.

This may seem like a bizarre story, but it's actually quite simple; loving yourself is the greatest way to improve yourself, and as you improve yourself, you improve your world.

It can change situations, past experiences, heal relationships beginning with self, and soften arguments. It is amazing what it can do – even my financial situation has turned prosperous in the last eight months of starting from when my soul guided me to hear it then use it. This was not a coincidence, just perfect timing again from soul.

It is a process that uses these 4 phrases, personalised to your story:

>   I am sorry / Please Forgive Me / I Love You / Thank You

Write the four phrases onto paper and memorize them. Think of your current situation and say them over and over, directing the phrases to yourself in a mirror is most powerful.

This is another example of the Prayer's answer which I wished I'd heard many years ago:

A woman worked at a terrible company and didn't know what to do. It was recommended that she wrote down all that she liked about working for the company, but she said she couldn't think of anything. She was asked, "Do they pay you a wage? Are the working hours convenient?" With a little encouragement, the lady went on to list the things she liked about the job.

When she was finished, she had to take each item off the list, look deeply into her own eyes in a mirror and say, "I Love My Job Because...." before each statement. She needed to do this a few times in the evening and before she went to work the next day and to continue this process throughout the week.

At the end of the week, she said "This incredible thing happened at work!"

Everyone was so amazed at the change in her, and the company changed so much that she now loves going to her job. By changing her own thinking and beliefs about her job, she changed herself and her attitude to the outside world.

> "Be the change you want to see in the world."

If you're having troubles in your own life, first try changing your own thoughts and beliefs and see if that helps solve the problem before you expect change from anyone else around you.

I personally used this prayer with great success, so I decided to share it with others. After any session of clearing core belief memories, I give my clients this prayer to reconnect to self. Whatever the youngest age is in the accessed memory, this prayer is said first thing in the morning and last thing at night, for seven days.

For example, if the memory was at eight years old, I would remember my little child's face, speak the prayer to her with unconditional love, from my heart to hers. Saying something at the end on of each phrase to reconnect. I also added an extra two phrases here. There are some examples beside the phrases but use what you feel best suits your own situation.

      I am sorry…… (you had to experience this)

      Please Forgive Me…… (for not trusting me to help you)

      I Love You…… (unconditionally)

      Thank You…… (for being so brave)

      I give you permission to…… (have fun, let go)

      I am very proud of you for…… (never giving up)

Your inner child has been separated and hidden from you for a very long time. You now need to mend the bridges within, reconnect to self and rewire your nervous system. The prayer makes it right within you by pulling all fragmented parts of you back together again. Follow what I have written and watch magic happen in your life!

The is the missing puzzle piece for many who have tried working with the Law of Attraction and have been frustrated when it seems it just doesn't work. I know we have so many unconscious and subconscious limiting beliefs that give us conflicting messages about whether we deserve to receive or are able to handle what life is offering us.

I'm sharing my knowledge for you to begin to be conscious of what hidden, sabotaging beliefs you are holding onto. These hidden beliefs will often make you feel like you have one foot on the accelerator and the other foot on the brake, stopping and starting. Hopefully by using this prayer, you'll start to see real progress.

I'd love to hear about your experiences with this prayer. If you'd like to get in touch, send me an email at:
bernie@innerchildharmonycoaching.com.au

***

When I began to love myself...

I began leaving whatever wasn't healthy for me, my mind and my body. This meant people, jobs, my own beliefs and habits, even some family members — anything or anyone who kept me small. My judgement called it disloyal. My heart saw it as self-love and self-compassion...

***

CHAPTER 11
MEDITATION – LETTING GO AND SURRENDERING TO SOUL

In this chapter, I'm going to take you through a meditation practice. We are connecting to mother earth and father sky, to the universal life force energy, throughout this meditation.

PREPARATION
- Allow yourself to get comfortable, preferably sitting, with your feet on the ground.
- Using Cedarwood or Frankincense Young Living essential oil, diffusing it or placing it on your crown or third eye chakra.
- Light a candle and have your journal to write messages, guidance and insights as they come to you.
- You can also record yourself speaking this meditation and play it back while you relax, or feel free to listen to me speaking the meditation on YouTube - http://bit.ly/2L0PFjH

Let's begin.

There are times in life when you need to hold on, there are also times to let go and surrender. Our mind keeps holding on to negative people, places and experiences which no longer serve us, but our heart and soul knows which ones to let go of. There is a place deep within you, where there is stored, inner knowing, inner wisdom, inner awareness. The more you relax, the more this place comes into your mind. Your awareness, your thoughts, your heart, every sound taking you deeper, every breath taking you deeper into your heart space, your Soul's space. Know you are safe, you are loved, and you are supported by soul, the universe, the divine in all things.

Imagine in front of you is a campfire of Soul truth, keeping you warm, safe and protected by the divine and you are surrounded by a bubble of light and love. Now bring your awareness down to your feet, down to the soles of your feet. Take a breath in and inhaling from the core of mother earth, up through the earth, through your feet chakra's (centre of foot), all the way up each chakra and exhale through your crown chakra (top of head) into the heaven's energy above. Relaxing the body as you exhale, knowing you are safe and divinely loved and expanding the bubble of light and love to surround your space where you are. Connecting below to above.

Breathing in from father sky, the soul's heaven, a deep cleansing breath, down through your crown chakra, breathing down through all your chakra's and out through the soles of your feet into mother earth. Relaxing the body as you exhale, knowing you are safe and divinely loved, expanding the bubble of light and love to surround you and your home. Consciously connecting above to below.

Take another deep breath in, imagining from earth to sky and back again, exhaling and connecting now above to below, you are now connected into your soul life force energy, expanding the bubble of light and love even more. Relaxing the body as you exhale, knowing you are safe and divinely loved, expanding the bubble of light and love to surround you cosmically. Connected by an infinity symbol, above to below to above again.

Place your hand on your soul heart, upper chest, connecting you to your inner child, helping you to connect deeper to self and soul.

When I talk about surrendering, you are not surrendering to someone or something outside yourself, you are surrendering to spirit within. You are surrendering to your higher self, your higher wisdom, to soul. Letting go, breathing in, scan now your relationships, your close relationships, your distant acquaintances and as you do this, is there any relationship that it is now time to let go of? Just see the people's faces, personalities, memories, just see them and let them float into the campfire of soul truth. Breath out and release anything or anyone holding you back.

We learn and grow from each other, but there are times and situations and people that for our own spiritual growth it is time to let go of. If you are aware of one of these relationships you might imagine the energy cords between you now dissolving. Wish that person well on their journey as that energy cord dissolves. Taking some time to do this – see the person and cords, see them dissolve. If you're not visual, just get a sense of them dissolving. Wish that person well on their journey and then let them go. Breath in pure love and peace, breath out old connections.

Scan situations in your life, maybe at work, maybe other situations. Are there any situations in your life that it is time now to let it go? Connecting with your heart and soul, allowing whatever and whoever is not for your highest loving vibration to be released now with love.

If there is any situation that you know, it can be large or small, see the energy cords between you and that situation, these are cords which connect you or attach you to it. Anything not serving, supporting, or loving towards you can now be released with love. Sense, see, visualize those cords dissolving, wish that situation well and let it go. Take some time now to complete this... Breath in pure love and peace, breath out old situations.

Scanning your life now, is there any situation or any quality within yourself, or a pattern of any sort that it is now time to let it go of? Self-sabotage, self-doubt, self-judgement, self-criticism? You do not need it anymore! If there is, visualize it before you, sense and see those energy cords, sense and see the cords dissolving, wish that quality, that pattern, that situation well and let it go. Breath in pure love and peace, breath out those negative vibrations.

There is great power in your ability to imagine, to visualize, to affirm. As you do this, you are becoming more and more free. Freedom fills your life, you've heard that expression "Let go and let god", "Let go and let spirit" whatever words you use for divine in the moment, let go and open your heart to the creator, open your heart to great spirit, open your heart to the universal life force within all things. You might imagine that you are holding you onto the shore, inside your vessel, you enter the great river of life, the great flow of the universe. Let go, let the creator fill you, let your soul guide you. You DO NOT need to do it all yourself. You do not need to do it alone, you do not need to control everything in your life. You are free to let go and let soul take over!

The more you do this, the more your deepest inner needs are met. For the creator knows those needs, you do not need to always fill all your own needs. You can indeed let go, soul is here, your creator is here. Your soul path and your life are divinely guided. Trust!

How would your life be different if you did let go? Imagine this – would you be more relaxed? Have more fun? Would you have more time with friends and family? Would you be wealthier? Happier and fulfilled? There is a place within you that knows, feel this new energy rising within you, filling all the emptied cells with this new divine energy.

As you are consciously dissolving those negative draining attachments, embarking on this change, trust that beneath your conscious awareness there is a powerful and profound surrendering. Surrendering to soul, surrendering to love, surrendering to light and surrendering to the creator! You are safe, you are free to surrender and let go. More and more a sense of freedom, more and more you know your life is divinely guided.

Allowing my words to be your words, repeating after me –

Who I am is enough for me.

I am safe to love and be loved.

My life is divinely guided.

I am safe to surrender to soul.

I am safe to let go of all that no longer serves or supports me.

My needs are met above and beyond my greatest expectations.

Breath in purest love and peace, breath out the negative residue. Now see the campfire of Soul truth, dissolve into the hands of god, the creator, see the hands close and disappear. What is done is done and cannot ever be undone! So be it!

Visualize now above you, the most radiant shimmering white light. Visualize this radiant light entering from the heavens above, down through the crown chakra (top centre of head), cleansing the darkness from each chakra downwards. Through the third eye chakra (between eyes), throat chakra (front of neck), heart chakra (middle of breasts), solar plexus (bottom of rib cage), sacral chakra (below belly button), base chakra (base of spine) then all the way down through the feet chakras into mother earth. Taking the residue of any darkness or negative build up and releasing it into the life force energy for transmutation.

Imagine now a huge crystal jug, filled with colours of the rainbow, these are your chakra colours we are renewing and refuelling. Adding to this jug, divine love, divine glue and divine honey, Love-Honey-Glue. When combined, the divine love fills up the neglected, depleted cells, the divine glue heals cracks, breaks and splits, while the divine honey is healing, sticky and holds all together, against the ego.

Allow this rainbow coloured, divine love-honey-glue to be poured from above, into your crown chakra, allowing it to fill all the chakras, covering the outside of the body and all energy fields as well. Allowing the violet colour to fill up your crown chakra with divine spiritual energy. Flowing down to your third eye chakra with the colour indigo, filling with divine inner knowing and wisdom. Next is blue for the throat chakra, filling with divine truth communication. Continuing to slowly pour into the heart chakra, the colours of green for healing and pink for unconditional love. Connecting to the divine source of all love. Next is the solar plexus chakra with yellow colour and filling with willpower and personal power.

Feeling fuller, absorbing all the divine loving energy, allowing your mind, body and chakras to receive this and more. Pouring now into the sacral chakra, the colour orange, filling up with creativity and expression. Lastly the base chakra, the colour red and filling with balance and foundation.

All energy fields are filled, your cup is now full and overflowing. Rest awhile in this abundant energy, allowing it to soak and absorb into all your cells, inside and out, this is all yours. Taking nice slow, deep breaths in and slowly breathing it out, you are safe, you are loved and fully supported by the divine.

Slowly coming back to waking consciousness, bring your awareness to your fingertips and toes, wiggle them, as you breathe in more pure, divine love and peace, breath out slowly. Taking another deep, slow breath of courage and confidence, sighing out any emotional residue. Thirdly, breathing in and allow all positive integration to take place across all times, all space and energy fields.

Rub the palms of your hands together for a count of ten. Hold them one centimetre apart, feeling the tingling energy between. Place the palms onto your eyes, to energise your eyes, hold for a count of five, then open your eyes. Take a new breath in.

Write your thoughts, feelings, answers and insights into your gratitude journal. Making sure you write a date beside the entry.

CHAPTER 12
WHEN I LOVED MYSELF BACK TOGETHER AGAIN

The more I clear myself of past negative programming and energies, learning the steps faster, the more life opens up and showers me with universal divine abundance in different forms. Connecting clients to me who also need guidance, clearing, healing, teaching and so much more. I am amazed at where they find my information; soul to soul channels.

I realized I had turned a chapter, closed the door on the self-made prison of my subconscious mind and broken the spell, curse I was under.

I changed the relationship within myself, mind and memories by re-connecting to my little self, my inner child. Standing up for her, protecting her, taking time to help her understand, telling her it wasn't her fault and she doesn't need to punish herself any longer.

I really listened to the stories and memories of my past, I heard the pain of my inner child wanting someone to find her but not trusting anyone to fulfil her wishes, even her adult self, me. Knowing how true these stories were at five years old, they should not be able to paralyse the adult life I lived, but they did. It is now 'safe' to release and replace with what I choose.

I re-parented my younger self, all of them who felt abandoned and orphaned, my heart was beginning to feel full again.

I stood up for all the younger versions of me, in memories hidden away. Each one didn't deserve to be treated that way, back then or ever again.

I could stand proud, speak my truth out loud, say, "Yes I did that. Yes it was me. Yes I want to do that. Yes, so what?" I didn't feel pressured into following someone else's dream and I felt ok, they would be ok too.

I could say 'No' and not feel guilted or shamed into changing my mind for others. How freeing and powerful is that? I can even sleep better.

I realized and was very grateful for knowing that in the darkest hours of my life, which there were many, my Soul was carrying me. Just as the story of the Footprints in the sand with God carrying the person, I visualize my Soul doing this for me. Soul has a purpose here on earth for me and I wasn't getting the message, I felt it was programmed and delivered to me in a different language, I didn't understand.

I can now laugh wholeheartedly at movies and events, when in times of the past, I cringed with fear or rage with the story deeply affecting me. Understanding the negative magnetic memory imprint was triggering my reactions, it is easy to dissolve and disconnect from those old memories to make new ones, I choose for me. And it is safe to do this now.

When I loved myself enough, I faced the many years of upsetting memories and stories that was my life in the past. I sat through the sadness, sobbing uncontrollably, the pain of my heartbreak and then I'd feel the grief of what could have been and never was. My body began to heal and repair itself miraculously because I allowed the whole emotion to be fully expressed and released from my body.

I was amazed at how my mind-genie had created perfectly on the outside, like a projector of old movies, whatever my buried core belief was on the inside, repeating until I took responsibility to change it for me. If the mind-genie was so strong and faithful for the negative beliefs, imagine when it was on my side with positive and supportive beliefs!

When I loved myself enough, I could manifest the best self-fulfilling prophecies of abundance, love, freedom, peace, with soul guidance lighting the way, so magical and so freeing.

I finally found that five freedoms came easily to my consciousness:

- The freedom to see and hear what is here, instead should be, was, or will be.
- The freedom to say what I feel and think instead of what I 'should'.
- The freedom to feel what I feel instead of what I 'ought' to feel.
- The freedom to ask for what I want, instead of always waiting for permission.
- The freedom to take risks on my own behalf, instead of choosing to be only 'secure and safe' and not rocking the boat.

Eyes wide open, I broke the spell, and could finally enjoy all of life, now, before my deathbed.

"As I began to love myself I recognised that my mind can disturb me and it can make me sick. But as I connected it to my heart, my mind became a valuable ally. Today I call this connection 'WISDOM OF THE HEART'. We no longer need to fear arguments, confrontations or any kind of problems with ourselves or others. Even stars collide, and out of their crashing new worlds are born. Today I know THAT IS 'LIFE'!" - Charlie Chaplin

***

When I began to love myself enough...

I deeply and profoundly loved and accepted all parts of me.

***

When I began to love myself enough...

I noticed and journaled daily, 5 things I did that day, that made me, proud of me! My life changed tremendously!

***

CHAPTER 13
LIVING A SOULFUL LIFE, EVER AFTER!

In 2015, I was called by Soul to return to Denise Linn's ranch in the USA to complete the Advanced Soul Coaching® and Past Life Regression courses. I had left the registration to the last minute, thinking there would be more courses on offer throughout the year, to my astonishment there was only one more advanced course, in thirty-two days' time.

So I said, "If this is what I am meant to do Soul, then show me the way and the money, make it happen." And what a whirlwind thirty-two days of ego mind-genie against heart and soul. I paid the deposit, booked the airline ticket and began to prepare for my trip, mentally, soulfully and physically.

I'd never had so many clients booked in and more calls coming in for appointments. When I had asked some clients how they'd heard of me, there were so many amazing stories, I could only say they were spiritually called to me.

This was Soul work, spiritually what I am called to do. But in the past, I had only ever worked within the physical and earthly realm, so I needed to trick my mind-genie and I repeatedly said, "If God was my employer what would he have me do?"

If Soul wants me to go to the USA, then I can trust the secretary angels will have the right flight and accommodation for me, I just need to trust and pay the money.

This was my mantra, almost hourly, to get momentum moving forward. The appointment book was filled, the money paying off the credit cards, all flowing easily, trusting and letting it flow. The week before leaving was the worst internal struggle, heart and soul against the mind-genie, I was very glad I had booked just thirty-two days before and not any longer.

I imagined I was driving a bus towards the USA trip and course, telling my mind-genie to get to the back of the bus, like it or not, we are driving through!

Each time I had negative thoughts come up, I would simply say, "Thank you soul, I have faith and trust in all that you do. God you are my employer, thank you for believing in me and thank you for this trip." Repeating over and over.

I made the trip, accommodation and course without any problems, reconnected to Denise Linn, my teacher and mentor for many years and other Soul Coaching® sisters and brothers. Giving gratitude and thanks to God as my employer for allowing me to attend, such a privilege and honour. So be it!

Since that trip, I use this mantra "If God was my employer, what would he have me do now?" and it opens my senses up to being present in the moment, seeing spiritually what I am meant to do, to be or be open to.

Soul has allowed me to learn even more about the Wounded Inner Child, healing more of my own self through the works of John Bradshaw and Debbie Ford. Being guided towards and now working with a Shamanic and Ascension healer, Raghida, Shaman. I have regular clearings of the negative residue from client's stories, allowing me to keep doing what I am doing in this Soul Awakening time of life.

With each client, I am able to assist them to access their deepest childhood wounds, connecting them to their many inner child memories being held hostage by their own subconscious mind-genie. Dissolving the layers and years of hardened emotional shutdowns, freeing them from living out 'the spell/curse' they have been under for far too many years.

The spell which keeps them in a downward spiral or a victim cycle they could not stop repeating.

My soul purpose is to help people overcome adversity and trauma to live an empowered happy life to the end of their days. To awaken their Soul purpose here while living on earth in the physical realm.

My life's reward is seeing, hearing and feeling the positive, loving changes which happen spontaneously and miraculously with each client. Sometimes I feel I am the Soul Godmother or the Wizard of Oz for clients who are called to see me. Helping them find the diamond within themselves, awakening their Soul to live life to the fullest before their deathbed. By changing their negative internal filters first, the world then changes around them by seeing through clear lenses, easily and effortlessly. This is a continuing evolvement of their heart and soul. Once they begin, it is a daily ritual to honour their self and their soul.

To keep your spiritual journey moving forward, and as my gift to you, [go here for your free The Journey™ eBook - http://bit.ly/2MQkWq1](http://bit.ly/2MQkWq1)

***

When I loved myself enough...

I learnt hurt people, hurt people.

Healed people, heal and change the world.

***

When I loved myself enough...

I received the love, fun, laughter and freedom I had always been seeking.

It was always inside of me, hiding.

***

ABOUT THE AUTHOR

Bernie Giggins is a Soul Coaching® and Journey Practitioner™ specialising in Core Belief Clearing for the Inner Child. Her soul purpose is to help people overcome adversity and trauma to live an empowered happy life, to the end of their days, with freedom and inner peace.

Her passion is helping clients break the cycle of bullying, abuse, burnout and compassion fatigue they are stuck in. She supports clients to move beyond their experience of past trauma. Her work enables them to develop inner strength and resiliency. This develops the courage to change their past circumstances, speak up, and move beyond their self-limiting beliefs to live a healthy, vibrant, and joyful life. Allowing balance and harmony to mindfully return to their life.

She is dedicated to helping empathic personalities and compassion fatigue sufferers understand and change their way of life, to regain their passion and satisfaction for their soul purpose in life to be carried out. To stay in their careers longer, receive satisfaction and be paid for their true worth.

Bernie experienced severe bullying, emotional neglect and sexual abuse from a very young age. This led to emotional shutdown, burnout, grief and bullying that continued into adulthood. It created patterns and behaviours that attracted abuse from toxic family members, old friends and within the workplaces.

Learning from mentors Denise Linn, International Soul Coaching®, Brandon Bays, The Journey™ method, Shaman Raghida, Inna Segal, Debbie Ford, and Shadow John Bradshaw, has given her a wealth of knowledge and wisdom to share with her clients. Bernie has sought the highest level of learning to access her own original unresolved childhood memories, where she found deep soul healing, forgiveness and freedom. She was able to discover her negative beliefs about life and dissolve the destructive patterns which drained her lifeforce. Changing her life direction from a bullying workplace to a soul driven, spiritual business practice. Over time Bernie has become the Soul Awakener for the Inner Child.

While one side of her life was in turmoil, the other side she held together, with her husband Laurie and has been happily married for thirty-six years. Parents to their family of three amazing children, Wayne, Jessica and Brett, their spouses Sonia, Adam and Jessica. She loves being 'nannie' to her six grandchildren who surprise her daily, Chase, Ava, Van, Jade, Chet and Eli, as she sees the fragments of her own lost childhood, now in her grandchildren, making her heart and soul sing with joy. She is forever grateful to her family for being beside her during the times she felt 'in a coma, under a spell or curse'.

Bernie is also a co-author and contributing author to Sibyl magazine, Holistic Bliss, 1000 Ripples and Soul Whispers III.

Today Bernie offers a wide range of coaching programs and services – from individual coaching to workshops and speaking sessions – including Core Belief Clearing, Soul Journey sessions, Soul Mentoring, Vision board workshops, Self-Compassion and Self-Love workshops, Declutter your Life course, 28-day Soul Coaching to your True Self courses and A Touch Of Soul Coaching Mentoring Program.

Connect with Bernie Giggins on her website - https://bit.ly/2JasqlE or Facebook page https://bit.ly/2zsAaji

The Journey method™
Seeing the truth through the light of your own soul, you can forgive yourself and others and heal once and for all in every aspect of your life. The Journey method will change your life forever. The first step is to have the willingness and courage to speak the truth of your own

direct experiences and come clean with your past. The memories are dissolved permanently, allowing you to move forward in your life with ease and grace.

I provide one-to-one personal sessions where you are guided safely to become the sacred observer of your younger memories, having the courage to change the perception and change your future life. I provide a safe and sacred space for this to happen, changing at the soul and cellular level.

We can settle for life as we have experienced it so far, with its limitations, pretences and suffering. Or we can wake up, stop the pretences and turn to face our fears. We can choose to look the tiger in the eye and realize it was always a paper tiger. We can finally become victorious and walk away feeling proud.

You do have a choice. You can continue to open up the old memory, talk about it, never healing it, like ripping the band-aid off an unhealed wound, or you can do something about it and never have to relive it again.

Get in touch with me today to get started - https://bit.ly/2u7vf1j

Soul Journey Core Belief Clearing

These sessions are a process of tracing back to the root cause of an issue, reconnecting to your needs required and permanently removing the past negative memories and positively changing the future direction of your attitude, behaviour, career and life in general.

Soul Coaching®

This is a powerful 28 Day program (undertaken over the course of 6 weeks). It is a thorough approach to de-cluttering the mental, emotional, spiritual and physical aspects of your life. This world-renowned program created by Denise Linn is comprised of daily, carefully designed, practical lessons which give you the tools you need to truthfully explore your life, challenge your limiting beliefs, face any fears, become even more self-motivated and inspired, bringing balance, harmony and clarity to a whole new perspective!

The program enables you to remove inner and outer clutter to assist you to re-define and re-Discover Your Authentic Self and hear the messages of your soul.

How Your Soul Coach Can Help You!

Do you know who you are and why you're here? Do you know what your mission in life is? Are you aware of the daily guidance from your soul? No matter how great your outer success is, if you do not know the answers to these questions, you might feel that something is missing in your life. That's where having a Soul Coach™ comes in. Your Soul Coach™ can work with you on many levels. In one-on-one sessions through a carefully crafted program, your Soul Coach™ can take you on spiritual inner journeys—Soul Journeys— into the depth of your soul to receive the answers to the heartfelt questions of your life. Most people say that these journeys are profoundly moving and transforming.

Is Soul Coaching like regular life coaching or like therapy?

Regular life coaching focuses on the attainment of a goal or dream; this differs from therapy, which is focused on emotional healing. Soul Coaching® goes beyond your emotions so you can connect with the wisdom of your soul. It's a spiritual experience in which the primary aim is to clear away your inner debris, so you can connect with the truth of your soul. Soul Coaching® allows you to be present—aware and awakened—in the joy of the moment.

Soul Services offered by Soul Coaches:
- **28-Day Soul Coaching® Program**—your Soul Coach™ is a personal guide for a total inner and outer clutter clearing of your life (individual sessions or group sessions/online or in person). This program is the heart and soul of Soul Coaching.

- **Soul Journeys:** your Soul Coach™ can take you on one-on-one individual guided journeys (and past life journeys) into the depths of your soul. This allows you to truly hear the wisdom of your soul and gain answers to the questions of your life (this can be done on the phone as well as in person.)
- **Vision Boards** – Creating the vision of your future to manifest. A great class with soul journeys and collecting pictures, meditations, sacred ceremonies, and celebrations.
- **Soul Coaching® Oracle Card Reading:** Using a special divination method that utilizes the wisdom in your Soul in conjunction with the Soul Coaching® Oracle Cards, your Soul Coach assists you in learning the answers to your heartfelt questions about your life.

Get in touch with me today to get started - http://bit.ly/2u7vf1j

Bernie Giggins has trained with me personally to become an Advanced Soul Coach and Past Life Regression Practitioner. She has an innate connection to the four elements through her work in this field. She truly makes a difference in the world by dovetailing her understanding of the four elements and her practice as an International Soul Coach to connect others to the truth of their soul.

– Denise Linn, author of Soul Coaching®, 28 Days to Discover Your Authentic Self, and Founder of Soul Coaching®

www.DeniseLinn.com

TESTIMONIALS AND CASE STUDIES

MY OWN TRAUMAS TO OVERCOME

TRAUMA BLOCK ONE: Losing My Hero
When I was thirty-seven, I received a horrifying phone call, early one morning, one I never thought would happen. My older brother, my hero, had been in a serious truck accident near his hometown. It was a nightmare. I was in shock, screaming, "Why take Patrick?!" He was just getting his life back together after huge health problems.

The whole family was in shock, waiting for the next call, hoping my younger brother got it wrong. He hadn't.

I had to work that day. My usual response to emotional pain was to shut it down. I rang work, told them about the accident, but I still wanted to go to work that day, I couldn't let them down. I was even going to let the kids go to school, what was I thinking? I didn't know how to deal with emotional pain, after years of emotional shutdown, I learned to sweep it under the carpet; don't cry, that's a sign of weakness and it'll make you a target.

I couldn't break free of this tangled web of unresolved and unexpressed childhood beliefs and memories still following me.

I stayed home, I was there emotionally for my family while I began to shut down and shut out, the usual disconnection not to feel the emotions.

His death and funeral were one we will never forget, etched in our memories, with our broken hearts for my hero brother, my husband's mate and my kid's greatest uncle.

"I have learned how the effects of grief and sadness, not expressed fully, stay in the body and can lead to depression, victimhood, self-

pity, loss of hope, blame, unhappiness and sickness. The negative feelings must be recognised and expressed in order to heal. It can be extremely difficult, each person deals with loss differently and time for healing is necessary. However, prolonged sadness and grief can keep you in focused on the past and limit you from moving forward."
– Inna Segal, The Secret Language of Your Body.

It was fourteen years after my brother's death when I fortunately learned The Journey™ method for clearing past traumas and allowing the body and life to heal back to balance. It took many more years for me to access this deep painful wound, as it was layered over by life itself, having the need 'to get on with life'. The soul will bring to the surface what needs to be cleared, only when the body is able to handle it.

With my valued Journey Practitioner beside me, together we travelled back in time to the memory which I had held in my broken heart. Seeing the memory bubble of the whole death, funeral and mourning stages, as if time stood still, I easily stood beside my broken hearted thirty-seven-year-old self.

As I watched the memory unfold this is what I saw...

Bernadette had hidden herself away, working harder (can be hidden, dark depression) to take her mind off this tragic event so she didn't have to 'feel' the painful feelings. She was able to finally connect to the soul of Patrick and speak all that she hadn't been able to say, with Patrick speaking back through spirit and on a soul level.

I am the future self - watching and connecting to my younger self, being mindful what other parts of the body are storing the grief, loss, and sadness. Bernadette realizes Patrick was the sibling who rescued her many times over her life in near accidents, advised her when she needed guidance, they shared a bond with each other's families and now he was gone. The memory also showed part of Bernadette had died with her brother. Asking with respect, the part that died, would it be willing to release and be set free. The answer was, 'Yes'.

Calling soul, god, spiritual guides, angelic realm and celestial beings to surround and protect the sacred ceremony for the release to be complete. Dissolving the tangled energies for Patrick to go to the light, for transmutation, allowing the soul to be free. Forgiveness, love and understanding for all sides, surrendering all heartache, permission to be released from all that is, emptying out all unspoken conversations and completing this memory. Allowing the younger version to come into the heart of the future self, to become one and united again. Then filling up with the positive, loving, supportive resources and new beliefs needed to move beyond this experience renewing the soul path.

The vision came forward of stepping out a grave, coming back to life, walking towards the gates of the cemetery and being cleansed spiritually. It looked like a fairy tale; Cinderella changing into the princess for the ball, magical and glistening sparkles dissolving this memory for good. When Bernadette walked through the gates, in front of her were her husband, all her children, spouses and grandchildren, as if they were waiting for Sleeping Beauty to awaken from this spell she had been under. Tears of joy and happiness, health and healing all taking place, by the grace of her God.

I could already feel the energy changes within beginning to work their magic.

From that day forward, Patrick's spiritual presence has really been made known to me. I feel the spell I thought I was in, all these years, had been finally broken and now I was able to express my true feelings whenever I needed. Freedom from different fears which had limited me have fallen away, allowing me to step into life more confidently. It felt like I was invisible and now people were recognising and complimenting me. How could this be possible? Because I had changed and healed the relationship I had within myself, not realising the real damage unresolved and unexpressed memories had over your life.

Looking back over the years, I felt Patrick had always been with me. The biggest shock, or wonderful surprise, after completing this Core Belief Clearing session, was when I was in America, visiting a Young Living farm. I was walking through a barn filled with majestic black Persian horses. Patrick and I had a deep connection in childhood with horses. As I was wondering through the barn, a song came on the radio which stopped me in my tracks. Tears welled up and I took a breath, hand on heart, it was a song from his funeral called 'The Last Dance' by Garth Brooks. I said, "Thankyou Patrick for being here with me, still keeping me safe." Miracles abound still, I feel, because I released the heartache, which had also kept his spirit here on earth with me.

Please note: Each client's journey session is different. They simply connect to their soul, the intuitive part of their being. I am here as their Soul Awakener, their guide, making sure their Inner Child is found, heard, the belief is replaced, and all is released from the bondage of the core belief memory. The lesson has been learned, the teachers released, the soul evolves to the next level, abundance flows, relationships begin healing.

Then through imagination and visualisation of their future, they fill up with positive emotion, so their mind-genie now knows what to seek out and bring forth, with effortless ease. Sometimes is maybe a past life, depending where the soul chooses to take us with the highest vibration of loving light. We go where we are intuitively guided.

TRAUMA BLOCK TWO: Losing Buddy
Our family dog, Buddy, was like the grandmother my kids never had. He was their protector while I was at work and gave unconditional love. He was part of the family, never just the family dog.

Buddy was 12 years old, he'd had a few bowel complications and over the previous couple of years and operations to relieve his health.

This time, Buddy was in severe pain, bleeding, and I needed to take him to the veterinarian.

The news was devastating. The vet couldn't do anything more for him and advised the humane decision was to have Buddy put down. Would I like to think about it first and then sit outside while they did what needed to be done?

I tried to phone my husband and eldest son, so I didn't have to make the decision. No one answered so I agreed. I sat there holding his paw, as if he was my child. Our whole family was heartbroken as he WAS our family.

A couple of months before Buddy passed away, I had learned a new modality called Reiki, energy healing. It helped me to connect back to my spirituality. I hoped it would support me with the bullying and intimidation I was suffering from at work and toxic family. Reiki helped me and my family so much with grieving our Buddy.

All pets are unconditionally loving, they simply want to take the pain away from their owner and replace it with fun and happy times. I remembered the many times I came home from work and would be stewing the conversations in my head, needing to make sense within myself before I spoke to others. Buddy would always be near me, head on my foot or lap, looking for a pat, hoping to cheer me up. I often wondered what he took on emotionally from me. If you have pets, notice how your pet treats you when you are upset, frustrated, angry, or sick.

Since studying compassion fatigue, I have learned this can begin to manifest in the person's life of anyone holding onto unresolved and unexpressed grief, trauma, loss, anger, bullying, abuse, from anytime in the past. Still being emotionally upset, even years later can be a sign of this lingering compassion fatigue.

When I was able to return to this memory, I thanked Buddy for all the love, support and protection he gave our family, for the time he was with us. I felt so relieved, free and so much lighter than the heavy blanket of grief, sadness and loss I had held onto since his death.

TRAUMA BLOCK THREE: Feeling Betrayed

I had arranged a party at my house and asked my parents and siblings to attend. They didn't show up. It was the worst let down and betrayal I had ever experienced, and it broke my heart.

On the day of the party, two years after my brother's death, I had spoken to my other brother and my mother who were the only ones able to attend. They were leaving and would see me that afternoon. Meanwhile I had been preparing for the party and feeling lucky they would arrive and be able to meet the friends we had gathered here for the party.

It was getting late in the afternoon and my mind started to wonder if they were ok. But, I corrected my thoughts, "Of course they are, not long now."

Some friends were arriving, and I thought I'd better call them to find out where they were and how long they would be.

They hadn't left the house yet and weren't coming. I was so angry at them. I swore into the phone, cried, then shut down the emotions. I didn't want to show our friends how let down I was by family.

My heart was racing for the next couple of days. I couldn't sleep, and I was sobbing and a mess. I felt my heart was broken and said to my husband "If I die, don't let them know. "If they can't turn up when I needed them the most, then I don't want them at my funeral!"

I felt better when I wrote a deeply moving, thankyou card, which was full of sarcasm to each sibling and parent. To my shock, instead of, "I'm sorry I hurt you" it was again, "How dare you". I soon learnt to write and burn/shred my feelings in Journalling.

Here we go again. The usual merry go round of conditioned punishment. Only this time my body was distancing itself from my ungrateful family, yet my head, my Ego wanted more. I still had the siblings close to me as allies and we supported each other throughout the years.

I wouldn't put up with another person doing this, so why do I put up with it from my toxic family? I would ask myself all the time. Yet the other half of me would give another excuse, give them one more chance, how many was that now?

Returning to this memory I felt in the pit of my stomach, felt like a punch in the belly. I also found there were other memories which were similar, where friends in my younger years at eight years old, played hurtful tricks on me; I still felt the pain of it. Once spoken out, released, forgiven and replaced with what I chose for me, the colour and texture had changed within my stomach. It is amazing how fast the body responds to the changes, once completed.

Afterwards I could talk about what had happened without any emotional reaction. It felt so good to be free of that memory to move forward in my life, instead of always fearing what might happen. It's like living life on hold, waiting to be told 'it's ok to risk or take a chance, you are safe to do this now', and that never happens – until you do this Soul Journey Core Belief Clearing.

TRAUMA BLOCK FOUR: Losing My Mother
My mother and father hadn't visited our home in eight years. We travelled to them all the time. My father was diagnosed in the January with an aggressive lung cancer, so we visited my parents again.

Then in May, I received the most crushing phone call I could ever receive. My mum had died of a massive heart attack. There were no more chances of having that mother-daughter bond. I had hoped to share time with my daughter and my mother, but it was not meant to be, so a part of me again shut down that day.

I was at work when the call came through and was in shock. I was the stores officer for the district, so I shut down my emotions again and kept working, finishing off the ordering for another couple of hours. I couldn't let anyone down, what would they think of me? My body was trembling with shock and I kept working, ignoring the shock and grief I was experiencing.

Soon after the funeral, my mother came to me in a dream, I felt we connected at the soul level and we spoke loving and soothing words. When we finished I helped her through to the light to be free. It was so surreal and an experience I haven't forgotten since. I knew I had to learn the Reiki for a reason and this was one of them.

Since then I have learned I had to face my biggest fear and core belief, 'I wasn't good enough to be loved fully by my mother'.

In my memory, I was that little five-year-old self, hearing the words, seeing the pictures, which I had stored in my broken heart. I finally faced and felt the sadness, rejection, abandonment fully, allowing my body, especially my nervous system, to release the grief through sobbing, shaking, and trembling. Normally I froze and closed my emotions but this time I knew it was safe and it was the right time to make peace, within me.

In this memory, my mind-genie had shut down and stored a lot of fragmented parts of my shadow or dark side ('dark' parts of us which are not accepted by others), which were not allowed to be seen or heard in front of my mother. On a soul level I could understand that my mother couldn't love all parts of me, according to her 'standards', but that didn't mean I had to hide them from the world.

That day, in that memory, I gave my little five-year-old self permission to be all that she chose to be and promised her she would be safe to share these gifts and talents with the world. She could speak her truth and release what needed to be said. Energy healing at the soul and cellular level was completed in a sacred soul ceremony. Re-parenting my inner child had begun.

After that Soul Journey Core Belief Clearing, my body was exhausted. I allowed it to rest and I slept soundly. I even had a beautiful dream with my mum coming to me, connecting lovingly, soul to soul. The changes the following day and beyond were more miracles. I was confident and proud to share with others all the parts of me I had kept hidden. I felt the love from my mother with more signs from heaven; I heard a song she loved, a friend gave me some roses (mum's favourites), I knew soul had broken the spell I had been under for too many years.

My need to have a closer mother-daughter relationship became an obsession after I had children of my own. I wanted my children to have what I never had, maybe my mother would connect with them and maybe I might get a crumb of her love. My egotistical mind wanted my mother to say, "You did a good job raising your family." When in fact, knowing what I know now, my heart had energetically closed at a younger age and even if mum did say or do something nice, the door of my heart was shut, unable to hear, feel or allow in, what she offered to me.

Many years later I realized my soul had given me access to a 'soul family' to fill my heart and needs up, with soul mothers, fathers, brothers and sisters. I had a surprise 50th birthday with family, friends and some of their parents here as well. Soul families are the spiritual family you have, not the earthly physical family. Soul showed me the soul mothers who treated me like a daughter but weren't my physical mother, there were also the soul father and soul friends walking alongside me through life and me not realizing their worth.

Ego, subconscious mind, wants what you cannot have, getting your attention with let downs, betrayals, broken promises, until you find and change the negative memory. When completed, that's when life unfolds in miracles and blessings, as a thank you from soul, your god source.

I have such a great connection to my mother now, speaking from the other side when I need her advice and guidance. Oh, the lessons I have learned at this stage in my life. My wish for you if this resonates with your life, is for you to connect with me, visit my website - https://bit.ly/2JasqlE and see how I can assist you to have freedom and inner peace in your life before too much longer.

TRAUMA BLOCK FIVE: My Father
It was not only my mother's negative influence it was also my father's.

Throughout the years, I couldn't trust my Dad as he was an alcoholic and bi-polar, manic depressive. When I wanted mum to attend my Naval graduation, she sent my dad instead, at other events the same thing. When I had my young family, my dad came to stay and wouldn't leave for weeks, he asked to borrow money and never repaid it, then he stole alcohol and money then lied about it, booked up items at local shops in my name which we had to pay for. In his manic states, I was extremely on edge, standing up to him took a lot of guts as he wouldn't listen to me about smoking in the house, among other things.

I even rang the mental hospital once and asked if they could help me as he wouldn't take his medication and I was worried for myself and young family. The psych nurse said they would come and talk to my dad, to which I freaked out. What if they took his word over mine, locked me up and leave my kids with him?

I hung up.

There wasn't any respect for my family from dad during those manic times and it was a nerve wracking time. What was mine, was his and what was his was his; his kids owed him for what he gave us.

This continued for many years, expecting more and being given less or being taken advantage of without permission. A part of me wanted my kids to have a grandfather in their life, he was better to them than what he was to me. The other part wanted to cut myself off from him as I had lost trust and faith in him, this all continuing the internal war zone in my head.

Since learning my new tools of Soul Journeying, I saw my father in the bigger scheme of life. I felt such compassion towards him and for what he taught me. I saw the reason why he was an alcoholic and possibly why he was bi-polar. He had firsthand experience with the deaths of his brother, when he was only nineteen years old, the deaths of my older brother, at 18 months old and a younger sister, only a day old, then the sudden death of his special younger brother. The heavy blanket of grief, guilt and shame which swallowed him, stayed with him his whole life.

I connected deeply on the soul level with the soul of my dad. With lots of emotional releasing from my heart as well as his, my heart which had been heavy was now getting lighter and brighter.

Days later, I could smell tobacco smoke and no one was smoking. It was dad's spirit here to connect and say it is all complete, the memory was erased. What is done, is done and cannot be undone, so be it! His presence is around when I need his guidance as well, I acknowledge him for all that he has done.

Life is sweeter when you know how to release these memories at the soul and cellular level.

CLIENT CASE STUDIES

CASE STUDY 1: Bullying and intimidation

Ellen, fifty-nine years old, an Executive of a large nursing home, was bullied and intimidated by other board members. She's now on stress leave, suffering health problems and being forced to resign. This core belief memory and fear continued to repeat throughout her life, after two marriages, she was now in a new relationship and had sought my services to find the root cause of this pattern.

The memory and core belief accessed went back to father issues – not measuring up to his high expectations at the age of seven. Ellen connected with several memories over her life repeating the same scenario. The present-day co-workers represented the personalities of her father and other dominating people from this childhood memory.

She was able to speak her truth, saying what was never said to her father, then releasing herself from this memory and replacing it by planting new seeds of abundance she chose for herself.

The result was a miracle. She had the courage to seek legal advice and took the company to court. The board was dismissed, and she was offered her position back again, which she declined.

Ellen's health improved, she continued to have a well-earned holiday with her partner and found a new positive career role.

CASE STUDY 2: Bullying, emotional neglect, and narcissistic family

Yvonne, fifty-eight years old, now a retired senior policewoman after twenty years, had thought her retirement years were for enjoying life. A small persistent cough had developed over a short time and the diagnosis was an aggressive tumour in her right lung. She chose natural alternative solutions to the chemotherapy offered, booking in for a detox clinic for alcohol, tobacco and sugar as well as Soul Journey Core Belief clearing sessions with myself.

The memory accessed was Yvonne at three years old, wishing this lung cancer illness to herself for attention. In the memory, she had visited a family friend with her parents, who was on oxygen therapy for emphysema. Yvonne's parents were so concerned and caring of the friend, they supported her constantly in the month's following, until her death.

She remembers thinking, "I wish I could be as sick, so I could get the same attention." Be careful what you wish for!

Being the youngest of two, Yvonne said, "It felt like three against one," for most of her life until now. Her core belief was 'Never being good enough for her parents'. Her family life was lonely with little emotional support and many volatile arguments. She felt she did well to survive a life with narcissistic parents and brother, however feared any confrontation.

She joined the police force "To make a difference to the lives of others, especially kids." She regretted her failed marriage (he had the personality of her father), and not having children of her own. She also had an underlying attitude of proving herself in this police field that didn't support her.

Connecting to her body wisdom, the aggressive tumour reflected how much she had neglected and denied her own needs for the sake of others. This is typical of Compassion Fatigue Syndrome – unable to disconnect to save herself.

After our clearing sessions, the tumour had slowed down, with the chemotherapy on hold. She learnt her health was number one and followed a daily routine of self-nurturing and self-care, finally able to make positive choices for her future.

CASE STUDY 3: Nursing intimidation, bullying, compassion fatigue
Annette, thirty years old, a senior nurse, was experiencing bullying and intimidation in her community centre workplace. She was suffering with stress, anxiety and depression, digestion issues and sleeping problems. Her clients were very needy and demanding, not taking the professional advice Annette was giving them. One client, who would not follow her requests, was making false complaints against Annette and her supervisors would not intervene because of short staffing.

This client was self-sabotaging, not taking the care of herself by following directions, and sometimes would physically abuse Annette during home visits. Annette felt she had no choice in her role and had lost patience with the management. The client would self-harm, which Annette documented, but no one supported her in this case.

During the Soul Journey Core Belief clearing session, Annette went back to six-years old when her mother, after years of self-harming, committed suicide, with Annette finding her body. She remembers several times, at her young age, rescuing her by calling neighbours or the ambulance. This memory had such a profound effect on her future life and was the reason she became a nurse. As with all Annette's clients, she became the little girl again, saving the clients, instead of allowing the client to want to keep themselves alive or improve their health.

As a result of our sessions, Annette changed careers, acknowledging and celebrating all her career achievements, knowing she did the best she could have done and had no guilt about the clients who had passed away. Her life was now full of enjoyment, passion, and a new sense of purpose, allowing self-love and self-compassion to be a daily routine.

CASE STUDY 4: Humiliation, scapegoat, bullying, intimidation

Gail, seventy-two- years old, was a retired teacher, had been married twice and has four adult children. Her health problems included problems with digestion, arthritis, stomach ulcers, knees and feet. She was still supporting two children financially and had asked for help to understand why she could not have an easier, stress free, healthy life at her age.

The memory accessed was of seven years old, at boarding school, which she hated. She was blamed for breaking something she didn't break. The teacher made her stand up in the front of the class and told the class 'Gail did it'. She felt humiliated, hurt and abandoned.

No one was there to comfort her that night and she was labelled a liar; no one believed her against the teacher. On weekends her parents did not come to take her home, making her feel like an orphan, unloved and unwanted in this cold, sometimes heartless boarding school.

She had kept this memory secret for sixty-five years and was one of the reasons she could not let her children suffer let downs of any kind, whatever the age. After the sessions, miraculously she cut back on the financial support given to her two children, allowing Gail to have a well-earned holiday. Her stomach and digestion problems which had related to feeling stuck in a pattern of fear, limitation, worry, guilt, judgement and criticism began to decrease.

Over time, Gail commenced a daily routine of meditation, journaling and being mindful of the messages her body was giving her. She was able to receive the help her children now offered to her and began to enjoy a stress-free life, finally.

After our sessions Gail said, "Thank you but where were you years ago when I needed you?" My answer, "You weren't ready."

CASE STUDY 5: Domestic violence, bullying, intimidation, no support.
Sally, fifty years old, married for twenty-five years with one child. She suffered four years of domestic violence. She and her husband were in a business together and he controlled the finances. The husband reminded her of her dominating, narcissistic and controlling father, who she never felt good enough for to live up to his high expectations.

Her mother did not support any decision Sally had made in her life which Sally felt emotionally neglected by. She could never expect any help from her parents in her decision to leave.

When she left her husband, she only had what she could fit in her car and she stayed at a women's refuge for as long as she was able to and then had nowhere, so she lived in a tent.

That's when she met me. Within twelve months of her sessions, Sally was able to access her superannuation fund to pay for legal costs and living expenses. She took her husband to court and won the case. He had to sell the property and business or pay her out, which he did.

Sally completed a business course, bought a new business and property in a different state. She has a new partner who loves and respects her. Her life has turned 360 degrees, and she is extremely grateful to have connected to her inner child and soul.

CASE STUDY 6: Client Who Escaped A Religious Cult
Karen, forty years old:

"I arrived at Bernie's office on my last legs physically and emotionally, utterly depleted after years of trying to heal from trauma. I hoped against hope that she would be able to help me, and that hope was rewarded far beyond what I could have imagined.

With gentleness and truth she helped me revisit damaging moments and people from my past, giving me a voice to speak my truth to them, helping me visualize my own little army of helpers so I wouldn't feel alone in facing those who had harmed me.

She provided a safe place for my body to react to those moments until all the pain was gone and I was left exhausted but at peace. The week after my first session I was astounded to discover that not only could I barely remember the events that had crippled me for decades, even when I thought on them, they had no power over me. In the past those memories had brought about vomiting, nightmares, full blown panic attacks, etc, but not anymore. They had been relegated to the past where they belong, no longer haunting me.

Bernie also helped me connect with my true self, my inner child, my spirit, my soul, whatever you want to call it. The trauma from my past had fragmented me, disconnecting me emotionally, physically, spiritually, mentally. As we worked through one trauma after another, those broken, terrified parts of me were healed and restored. It was like a reunion and I have felt more and more whole, less and less alone.

It's only been six months, but the growth and healing I've seen and experienced make me smile and cry with gratitude. I'm finding my voice, learning to stand up for myself, sleeping through the night, able to connect with others in a healthy, loving, and strong way. I see myself as an equal now, not a slave or servant or victim. I am more and more comfy in my own skin, able to close toxic relationships and thrive in healthy ones.

After 40 years of traumatic events, I know my healing journey will take time, but I no longer fear that journey because I know that healing, peace, and contentment are on the other side of each session. That gives me courage."

CASE STUDY 7: Love, guilt and grief

Leah was only seventeen years old when she moved from her country town to the city to begin a new career. She had left behind family and her boyfriend, James. She returned home once a month, sometimes fortnightly depending on her roster, and they sometimes visited her.

It was now Leah's 18th Birthday, and James had decided to pay her a surprise visit. Meanwhile, friends had taken her out to dinner to celebrate her birthday. He waited patiently until she returned home about 11.30pm. Leah was intoxicated and very talkative, not wanting heavy conversation. They had an argument, he said, "I may as well leave" to which she agreed. So, he left on his motorbike at 12.15am and she went to bed.

At 2.30am she was woken by a phone call from James' hysterical mother saying James had been killed in an accident on his way home.

That memory has been locked into her subconscious mind for thirty-one years. The emotions still unresolved, not able to say "sorry", not able to speak about how she felt. The memory she thought she had dealt with was still alive and had been driving her behaviour ever since.

She'd never had a relationship of more than 2 years. She was very petite, with lung problems and unable to give up smoking.

During our Core Belief Clearing Soul Journey Sessions we uncovered the buried memory of that fateful night. The body remembers everything and never lies.

The 18-year-old was still sitting there in grief and shock inside her right lung. Which we accessed through her body wisdom. She was nervous, anxious, on antidepressants. The belief uncovered was, "It's my fault, if I hadn't gone out drinking, if only I had not said what I did – he would still be here."

She felt she didn't deserve to live. "If only" now ruled her life. James died that night and Leah's heart died along with him. Whenever she felt confident and happy, her old limiting negative belief would push away or sabotage any new beginning. Pushing her back into sadness, self-doubt, self-loathing, not wanting to live. She would sometimes sleep on his grave when she went back to her home town.

Leah had been paying a life sentence for her mistake, until her sessions released her from this curse. We did a Soul to Soul Completion Ceremony where we call the soul of the departed into the session. The heart of Leah speaks and empties out her grief, anything unsaid and whatever else the body needs to express. James' Soul replied, "It's not your fault, it was my time to leave. I have been with you all this time, watching you."

12 months later she has met her soul mate, Keith, who cherishes Leah. Their love is something Leah has not felt for 31 years. She is released from this old outdated belief and is making up for lost time. Inner peace and happiness now fills her life daily, making up for lost time.

Keith and Leah plan to get married in 6 months' time. She now realizes the importance of clearing the emotions not said through the day, week or month. She meditates and expresses through any means – her favourite is to dance!

James is still around, and she communicates with him often. Everyone comments and compliments Leah; her smile and new energy is very noticeable.

CASE STUDY 8: Teenage Love Heartbreak

Kareen was in her 40's and presented with depression and anxiety. She had feelings of being unheard, not good enough, without direction or motivation. She had gained 20kgs in 9 months and suffered from migraines and panic attacks.

Physically seeing into her energy field, I could see she was only taking up a quarter of the size. Three quarters of her energy field was everyone else's expectations of her, responsibility to others in her roles – wife, mother, daughter, sister and friend. As if they owned her energy. She was a slave to others and needed to be there for everyone's needs while her needs came last.

From an early age, Kareen began to offer help to others, then offered even more help as she was getting acknowledged and was valued by these people. Something inside her would not allow her to stop. She just kept giving more time and energy to others. This was taking her further away from her own needs and planted the seeds of depression, not being able to speak her truth and stop.

Eventually the pattern replaying caused her to either have a migraine, or depression set in. Worse still, she suffered a panic attack and needed hospitalisation or medication.

I call this pattern 'smell the cheese' – if we're not aware of the negative behaviour, soon it will be the rat trap coming down on our head.

The memory that showed up in our session was of 15-year-old Kareen. Her boyfriend of two years had left her. The unresolved emotions of sadness, loneliness, hurt and rejection were still there inside her body as if someone had closed the door and sealed it up. The rejection had seeded a belief she took on about herself that she was not good enough for his love. This seed has been growing inside this closed, sealed room inside her heart, which oozed negative energy into her life.

Seeing into her younger self's heart, it was frozen at the age of 15 years. This small, locked, frozen part of the heart said, "No one gets to touch or break this heart again." That belief became a vow and the vow became the story of her life. She had to play out the 'not good enough for his love' belief by being more than good enough to others. But it didn't matter how many times she did this, nothing filled that void. That endless hole of 'not being good enough'.

The Inner Child Core Belief Memory only stops the repeating pattern/cycle when you, the adult, stops it. Become aware, trace it back, face it, erase it and replace it. Re-parent your younger self, give yourself what you never received back then, and begin a new routine of feeding and nurturing your own needs. This allows others to do the same.

This is 31 years later and she is still crying over the memory. She will see males with a similar appearance to him, never having got over him. Meanwhile she has been married twice and has four children to two fathers.

Her sealed up frozen heart at 15-years was waiting for her boyfriend to return and open the door, so she could love and live again. Self-loathing, self-inflicting harm by drinking, shopping, over eating and constantly pleasing others was taking its toll on her body and her life.

It looked like her heart died that day. It was sealed in Davey's Locker and the key thrown away. Submerged in the ocean, only to be found and opened by this boyfriend – who could never be found.

The toll this negative core belief and memory had on her body was very sad to see. In the stomach was an endless river of how many people she served, had given away to, not able to hold onto the little she received back, with nowhere to hold it or store it.

In her heart was a scene of mourning the death of her life she had dreamed of. Her boyfriend's shrine in the centre, replaying their relationship like a movie. At 15 years old, she glorified him. They were going to get married and have children, and this was their dream, together. Then he ended it by walking away.

"Now I'm going to make me suffer" was the promise Kareen's younger memory made.

This young memory isn't dead, she didn't get over it, it stayed buried inside the deepest, darkest, loneliest part of her subconscious and has been driving her behaviour since. Causing the health problems, depressive emotions, and roller coaster ride of her life until now.

Unlocking the door to this memory allowed it to be found, opened, removing the negative emotions and filling it up with forgiveness, love, and compassion.

She could feel the confidence and inner strength beginning to circulate and the connection to herself had been restored. The love of self-had returned and she had steps now to take each day to keep this connection in place.

She was back in alignment with herself; her own needs and desires were the most important. Now the feelings on the inside reflect to the outside, people and life will treat her how she treats herself – with love, trust, and compassion.

CASE STUDY 9: Sexual, physical and emotional abuse

Iris is 45 years old, single and separated from her husband with an 18-year-old son. She now works in a State Child Safety & Protection branch overseas.

Iris had an ovarian cyst, renal problems, chronic urinary tract infection, chronic thrush, and gallbladder and psychiatric symptoms from past physical illnesses.

Her ex-husband had domestic violence orders to have no contact with Iris or their son, who he had molested. Because of this, Iris had changed identity and moved away for her safety. Iris has changed names and moved with a new identity three times in total.

She has a deep hatred for her mother and brother and has excluded them from her life. The dilemma is now her son, at 18, wants a relationship with his maternal grandmother. This is a huge shock and hurts Iris deeply.

When younger, she felt safer on the streets, in nature, or at school than she did in her family house, not home. Her brother was 18 months older and dominated and overpowered Iris. He was the 'golden child' and supported by their mother.

Iris' belief was "I'm not heard, I don't matter, I have no voice and I don't exist." These beliefs have played out in her life.

She has a hereditary family history of repeating sexual patterns. Her paternal grandmother was a persecuted Jew in the war. Iris's father was born illegitimately and sexually abused as a child. Shame, guilt, and persecution had been running through the family lines for many years. Iris then suffered sexual abuse by her father as a child and her mother left him when Iris was 6 years old. Later in life, Iris's husband sexually abused their 5-year-old son and Iris separated from him, changing identity and moving interstate.

Iris's mother had dated many boyfriends and when Iris was 7 years old, her mum brought home another one. This one was a paedophile who hung around Iris's school. He molested Iris's friends who had gone with them both as they trusted her. Iris knew what happened but couldn't protect herself or her friends. She told her mum who believed the boyfriend. There was no one listening or standing up for this little 7-year-old girl who was the innocent one.

When speaking to Iris's body wisdom in our session, the health problems were manifested from the old unresolved emotional issues of the past. Within 6 months, some of the health challenges had subsided and with more Soul Journey and core belief clearing sessions planned, Iris was feeling more confident in herself and her life in the future. She could see how her 'inner child' had been rescuing and saving so many other children and why she was dedicated to her career role in child safety protection. She was now able to be discerning with her workload, taking time for herself to heal and create a balanced life that suited her.

CASE STUDY 10: Sexual abuse

John, forty-five, had been on prescription medication for severe depression for many years. He worked as a counsellor in a helpline call centre for children. He worked long hours with extra shifts due to staff shortages and was dedicated to his job. He was suffering burnout and compassion fatigue. Over the years he had tried many forms of therapy to uncover the cause of his depression and health problems.

The memory accessed was at four years old. A friend of the family who was living in the home, had sexually abused John until he was nine years old. He had threatened John many times 'not to tell anyone or he would hurt John's pet cat'.

Within the core belief clearing sessions, John was able to connect with his four-year-old self, speak his truth, seek the love and protection from his parents and clear the negative core belief. By re-parenting his own inner child, he released the belief of it being his fault, and gave permission for his body to heal the scars of these old memories.

Over time, John was able to discontinue his medication, with the doctor's permission and amazement at John's change. He was able to enjoy life again, filled with trust and love. His relationship with his wife was the best they had ever experienced. The new relationship with himself allowed the outside world to match, in positive and supporting ways, which was a new change he is still getting used to.

He chose a better work–life balance, being able to disconnect from his job after hours by following a daily self-compassion and self-care routine. His life continues to improve by enjoying overseas travel for the first time and being open to new experiences all the time.

CASE STUDY 11: Rape, guilt, shame, humiliation

Beth had been married three times and within each marriage, the husband was unfaithful. She had two grown up children, suffered back and weight problems and was turning fifty. The most traumatic memory accessed was at seventeen years old, while living with a girlfriend, a man broke in and raped Beth while her friend was locked in another room. Later in court, the whole scene was aired publicly, stirring up the raw emotions once again.

To her horror, as well as her family, the verdict was 'not guilty'. Beth plunged into anxiety, deep depression and was medicated. The family appealed and went to the higher courts, repeating the same emotional pain and again the verdict was 'not guilty'.

This memory had closed and etched into her subconscious mind for all these years. Together in this memory, we found her seventeen-year-old self, which had spiritually died and buried herself in a cemetery grave. If two court cases, with all the public humiliation and shame, did not believe her then she may as well die, so in the memory she did.

Beth re-connected and re-parented her younger self, releasing and dissolving the old core belief and memories associated, replacing them with new seeds of hope, trust, faith, freedom, joy, and happiness.

Beth had dedicated her life to supporting young adults going through the court systems and didn't know the underlying reason why, until now. Since then, Beth is now teaching them spiritual and emotional techniques to heal their lives, to move forward. Her life is so much more relaxed, open and loving, her children have noticed and love the new energy surrounding their mum. She is loving the changes which have already occurred and continues with her daily routine of self-care and self-compassion.

CASE STUDY 12: Grief and Failure

Anne, forty-eight, could finally access a deep layer of grief, pain and shame, which was plaguing her life. Anne had five births with only two children surviving. As a young mum, her first three pregnancies resulted in the babies dying in utero the later stages of pregnancy and before birth. Back in the nineteen sixties in a small country town, they didn't have the grief counselling and support they do now. She just got on with her life and the next two pregnancies were healthy boys. In her teenage years she was kicked out of home by her mother and new boyfriend and did not have the mother connection for support.

Anne overtime smothered them with love and protection, spoiling them by giving them everything they asked for and more. One of her son's rebelled by taking drugs in his teenage years, the other in trouble with police. Anne took this as another failure to parenthood and sought help. We discussed her repeating patterns and timeline and found the broken heart of the young mother. Together we did a Soul to Soul reconnection process, to speak to each of the souls of her little unborn babies, releasing what was not able to be said to them at that time and understand their lesson in life.

This brought peace, forgiveness, and healing back to her heart, body, and mind. She understood the reason why she became obsessed with her two sons, feeling a failure as a mum and forgave herself. Re-parenting of herself and the sacred ceremony was completed. Afterwards, the love between her husband and boys was the deepest she had ever experienced. Her heart was now opening to receive, as it had been closed for many years.

Anne has since had her own grandchildren bringing in more love for her to cherish. Her sons were beginning a new direction with children of their own, undergoing counselling for their addictions with Anne supporting them, not doing it for them.

She continues to receive miracles and blessings in her life which she is so grateful for.

CASE STUDY 13: Lung and Brain Cancer
Dianne, forty-nine years old, had lung cancer which spread to her brain. During the sessions, she accessed two major traumatic events. First was at nine years old, not able to live up to her father's expectations and dominating rules. He was in the army, for which they had moved locations many times. She was the eldest of four and had to care for her younger siblings to help her mum. She felt she was never good enough in the eyes of her father, no matter what she did. We cleared and changed that.

The second memory was at twenty-five years old. Dianne was living on and sailing a yacht with her boyfriend. She had left for a week to attend a birthday party; her boyfriend ran the yacht aground and was killed. Dianne had to return to retrieve what was left. She felt it was her fault and responsibility for his death.

When asked what the relationship was like, Dianne reported it was filled with domestic violence and she had to work harder than her partner, who had her father's personality. This memory was stored in her lungs. She cleared and replaced it with love, healing and gratitude. She now understood that her soul had sent her away to the party because if she had stayed, she would have ended up dead herself.

The result was a much better quality of life with her young son and husband. She could now sleep without fearing death and enjoy life together one day at a time. Dianne, her husband and son were extremely grateful for the change to their lives, while it lasted.

CASE STUDY 14: Vertigo Prevents a Fulfilling Life
Tom, thirty-eight years old, had suffered from vertigo for the past ten years and could not drive. For the first five, he was unable to leave the house, after that, he had a mate give him a lift to his work.

He and his wife needed to swap roles; he became the house husband and father to three small children, while the wife was the breadwinner with full time work for the first five years.

During the sessions we discovered that Tom had witnessed his father beating his mother in alcohol fuelled arguments in his young life. He tried to stop the fights but was pushed away. His father left the home when Tom was only four. Tom became the 'man' to look after his mother and young sister he was the protector and trusted problem solver – this was his core belief.

Ten years ago, within twelve months, three mates had either been killed or took their own life. Tom didn't realize how much this had weighed on his mind until these Core Belief Clearing sessions. One mate was killed in a car accident, while the other two had taken their own lives. The last and one of his best mates, Chris, had taken his life the night before Tom and his family were to leave for trip to holiday with him and his family.

Through the night, not knowing Chris had taken his life, Tom had a dream where Chris had said, "I can't take it anymore, I'm out of here, let me go." They had a fight with Tom telling Chris to 'wake up to himself and stop mucking around.' He didn't think too much about it until Chris's wife rang to tell him about the horrific news. A note had been left with read exactly what Chris had said in the dream to Tom. Tom asked what Chris was wearing and it was the same clothes he had seen in the dream.

After the funeral, Chris again came to Tom in a dream, this really freaked Tom out. Guilt set in that Tom didn't do enough to stop Chris ending his life, and many more intrusive negative thoughts led to continual sleepless nights.

Over a few months insomnia and anxiety crept in. The doctor prescribed medication and he thought his mind would settle down.

His next health problem was vertigo, which confused the doctors, but additional medication was given to help settle this.

It didn't. Over the ten years he visited many specialists, underwent numerous tests and nothing changed.

Fast-forward ten years, Tom was able to go back to what happened before the vertigo in his timeline and connect with the different memories and his inner child. He was shown how special it was to have his best mate appear in a dream, to be released and set free, instead of being freaked out.

He said what needed to be said after these many years, hearing back what these mates needed to give him. By being open spiritually to see the whole picture, he was able to release the grip these memories had over his life, shutting him down from being independent. He allowed his inner child to release the responsibility he had taken on to be the protector and trusted mate to everyone, except himself.

Within four weeks the vertigo had subsided, he had to wait another couple of weeks for clearance from the doctors to drive again, and miraculously he was free. He was able to drive to work again and the family changed roles. His wife and daughters loved his new energy. He was able to the things he hadn't been able to do in the past ten years, by getting out and traveling with the whole family. Tom has learned meditation and journaling to enhance his new-found spirituality. Life is great again.

CASE STUDY 15: Suicidal Client
Katie, thirty-nine years old, had tried to take her own life and had reached out for my help. She was a hard-working wife, mother of three and managed the family's large property. Life had been tough; breakdowns of equipment meant more money to fix or replace and finances became worse with no rain for a few seasons. Her husband worked away in the mines and there were no families nearby to call

upon for assistance when Katie needed it. They had taken out a car lease loan and Katie was beginning to stress over the repayments, along with anxiety creeping in. Katie worked harder so as not to let anyone down, especially her husband and children.

More bad news came when another water pump breakdown spiraled Katie into severe depression. She was not able to sleep with her mind racing with controlling thoughts. She had thoughts of suicide and tried overdosing on tablets.

Through our sessions, we uncovered childhood memories of watching her parents going through the same situation and losing their property.

Katie's past fears and unresolved memories were now re-creating, repeating, making Katie relive the same scenario, until now.

Because Katie had removed the unexpressed emotional memories, she felt a huge burden had lifted, one she could now speak freely about. The result was a new outlook on life, seeing things through new eyes, communicating her needs to her husband and friends, allowing people to help when needed, and her parents were more involved. Taking time pampering for herself regularly and having family holidays away from the farm.

Looking at the experience, there wasn't any real problem with the financial repayments, only the perceived problem of 'what if' something went wrong. This linked back to the unexpressed memory of her parents' financial problems.

Journaling became her best friend throughout her healing journey back to self-love and self-compassion. Twelve months after, I received a thank you letter from Katie for helping her connect back to her inner child and releasing the old memories. Her life has been amazing since and she is so grateful she didn't take her own life.

Case study 16: Lack, struggle, limitations

Diedre, 59 years old, divorced Mother of Two, had an obsession with paying bills on time and being prepared. Her daily house duties include cooking for herself with plenty of cakes and biscuits. If her adult children, son or daughter, are busy at work or sick, Diedre will bake for them too.

We were discussing the "need" to pay on time or before the due date, never wanting to let someone down or be fined. Diedre discovered a memory as a 13-year-old teenager. Within this memory Diedre had stolen a packet of biscuits to eat as she was "starving". She felt guilty at the time for stealing them and worse for not sharing them with her siblings. This created a quandary within her mind, if she shared the biscuits someone would dob on her to their parents. If she was found out she would certainly be flogged as a punishment.

The family of seven had it tough and worse still Diedre's parents locked up the pantry and fridge and rationed the food for the children. Her mother had a "stash" of the best biscuits hidden for herself while her father could still have his smokes. This was not the right way to raise children, ration the kids while the parents could still have their luxuries and it was a confusing time for Diedre.

Her home wasn't a good place, she didn't feel loved, accepted, or safe. She felt there wasn't the support, affection, or encouragement she needed to belong and hoped one day it would change.

She'd kept this secret alive for forty-Six years and now realizes why she automatically "does the things the way she does". The core belief, pattern and habit created at 13years old was "to survive, you need to do what is right for you. My parents are not concerned for my welfare, I need to look after me, steal, lie, whatever it takes!"

Still subconsciously believing she will be in trouble, found out, she repeated the same behaviours as her childhood. All the times over her life the same "scenario" had been re-created, to have the same result or outcome.

Your conscious adult self has normal goals, dreams and want to be successful, happy, financially independent, have a satisfying career, have a reliable loving spouse or partner, but if it doesn't fit the "image" to match what your core belief, there's a problem.

Your subconscious mind will start self-sabotaging, self-doubt, self-judgement to betray your word. The deepest core value, belief, life commitment is in control of us. We will always act in accordance with this commitment - no matter what.

Diedre has now brought forth all other similar memories. Together we cleared, dissolved, and deleted in a sacred ceremony, disconnected at the soul and cellular level.

Diedre was able to see how her character and motives made her act as a scavenger, hiding, sneaking, binge eating. All these related to her old core belief/life commitment, but now no longer in her DNA, she is free.

Diedre now is refilled with new energy of self-worth, self-value, self-love and so much more. Her adult self-congratulated her on doing what she needed to do to survive, thanked her for staying strong and passing these lessons onto her children and grandchildren. She is a wonderful mum and role model because of her childhood and the younger teenager was finally recognised, acknowledged, and rewarded. So many memories were replaced with optimism, adventure, honesty and now integrity.

Six months later Diedre is slimmer, happier, enthusiastic in her life, seeking fun and laughter without the "addiction" to overeating or paying bills early. Her family and friends love this new Diedre and she has no plans to put her back in the closet.

MORE TESTIMONIALS – Emotional Clearing of negative memories

Craig - https://bit.ly/2KKOeKe Surviving Mental & Psychological Abuse

Sanela - https://bit.ly/2zmONEw   Surviving a Genocide

Karen – audio - https://bit.ly/2L4foYy   Surviving a Cult

Mary – audio - https://bit.ly/2L4W0e3   Surviving family neglect & abuse

Testimonials are always being added to My YouTube Channel, use this link to Subscribe - https://bit.ly/2NGDSsy

Book Reviews:

'Practical help to resolve inner emotional turmoil. Confronting, challenging and yet hope-filled to know there is someone who has walked the walk before, been there, done that and survived. Thank you for your insight into childhood trauma and practical help to resolve inner emotional turmoil.'   Denise Hart-Christie

'A search for inner peace, happiness and love. This statement "because of this we live life doing for others what our inner child yearns to have done for us" spoke volumes to me, allowing me to consider what it is that I unconsciously do for others that in reality I would love to have done for me. - An eye opener of just how powerful our unconscious conditioning can be. The author shares her deepest most personal experience that I am sure most readers will relate too. This book is filled with lessons that must not only be read but be applied daily. Highly recommended.' Brenda Tsiaousis

I would appreciate it if you would please send your review of HEAL to bernie@innerchildharmonycoaching.com.au

Website: https://www.innerchildharmonycoaching.com.au/

www.ingramcontent.com/pod-product-compliance
Lightning Source LLC
Chambersburg PA
CBHW072047290426
44110CB00014B/1582